Look Inside!

Common Misspelled Words Practice

Spell each of your words by looking carefully at the spelling, covering the word up and then try writing it by yourself.

A Lot	AWhile	About	Absence	Academic
Accept	Access	Accidentally	Accompanying	Accomplish
Accomplishment	According	Accordion	Accurate	Accuse
Ache	Acquaint	Acquaintance	Acquire	Across
Activities	Actual	Adapt	Address	Adjacent

Carefully circle the correct spelling combinations of words.

	A	B	C	D
1.	Suite/Sweat	Suite/Swet	Suite/Sweat	Soite/Swet
2.	Tame/Thyme	Time/Thye	Time/Thyme	Tame/Thye
3.	Intense/Intents	Intense/Intents	Intense/Intents	Intense/Intents
4.	Packed/Pactt	Packed/Pact	Paked/Pactt	Paxed/Pact
5.	Allode/Elude	Aluda/Elude	Allude/Elude	Alode/Elude
6.	Rheum/Rom	Rheam/Rom	Rheum/Room	Rheum/Roum
7.	Rowed/Road	Ruwed/Rod	Rowed/Rod	Ruwed/Road
8.	Duel/Dual	Duel/Dual	Duel/Daul	Duell/Daul
9.	Chote/Shot	Chute/Shout	Chute/Shoot	Chute/Shot
10.	Mist/Missed	Mist/Mised	Mist/Misced	Mist/Miced
11.	Faintt/Faint	Faintt/Faint	Feint/Faint	Fient/Faint
12.	Faon/Fawn	Faun/Fawn	Faun/Faw	Fuan/Fawn
13.	Fryer/Frair	Fryer/Friar	Fryer/Friar	Fryer/Friar
14.	Arck/Arc	Arrck/Arc	Ark/Arc	Arcle/Arc
15.	Ilacit/Elicit	Illicit/Elicit	Ilicit/Elicit	Illacit/Elicit
16.	Yew/Ewe	Yew/Ewe	Yew/Ee	Yew/Ee
17.	Taad/Tide	Taid/Tide	Taid/Tide	Taad/Tide
18.	Forth/Foorth	Forth/Fourth	Forth/Fourth	Forth/Foorth
19.	Morning/Mourning	Morning/Moorning	Morning/Mourning	Morning/Mourning
20.	Rutte/Wrote	Rutte/Wrote	Rotte/Wrote	Rotte/Wrote

Underarm	Keypunch	Moonshine	Dogwood	Earthbound	Newsstand
Sundown	Newborn	Sisterhood	Headlight	Moonwalk	Upright
Blackout	Spacewalk	Turnaround	Whitewall	Skylark	Earring
Toothpick	Whitewash	Sometimes	Comeback	Daybed	

1. ANNJJURORTD   T _ _ _ _ _ _ u _ _

2. STHSEORIOD   S I _ _ _ _ _ _ _ o _ _

3. REDRAUNM   _ n _ _ _ _ _ _ m

4. SKALRYK   S _ _ _ l _ _ _

5. HWA LEITLW   _ _ i _ e _ _ _ _ _

6. LMWKOOAN   _ _ o _ w _ _ _

7. WBRENNO   N _ _ _ _ _ n

8. DUTTNAOS   _ _ s _ _ _ f

9. BAYDED   _ _ y _ _ d

10. IRENRGA   _ _ r _ _ _ g

11. KTTOIPH OC   _ _ o t _ p _ _ _

12. DOOW ODG   D _ _ _ _ o _ _

13. ITSEMESOM   _ _ _ e _ _ _ _ s

14. MCCBKAOE   _ _ m _ _ _ _ k

15. PCY UHKEN   _ _ y _ _ _ c _ _

16. TOAH LEGHI   _ e _ _ _ l _ _ h _ _

17. UDHREOABTN   E _ _ _ _ _ o _ _ n _

18. H IWHWSETA   _ _ i _ e w _ _ _ _

19. HSNOENIMO   _ _ _ _ _ _ h i _ _

20. EACLASWPK   _ _ _ _ _ _ w _ _ f _

21. SNNDUOW   S _ _ _ _ _ p _

22. SD WASNTEN   _ e _ _ _ _ _ a _ d _ _

23. RGIUTPH   _ p r _ _ _ _ _

W	S	O	L	X	A	I	D	O	K	S	F	X	D	R	A	M	K	H	X
S	U	P	O	R	H	V	M	A	N	D	T	V	G	E	R	V	K	A	T
O	W	R	U	P	R	I	S	I	N	G	E	R	W	A	D	T	W	N	G
Q	B	U	R	L	G	U	P	T	U	R	H	D	O	U	R	O	C	D	P
V	U	P	C	X	R	K	E	Y	W	A	Y	U	E	R	R	W	I	M	R
H	T	E	A	S	P	H	R	J	S	C	T	S	Z	B	U	T	J	A	S
E	T	R	R	B	E	N	O	M	L	I	O	E	S	S	F	H	M	D	L
U	E	S	P	I	R	B	A	Z	I	M	T	O	L	R	O	T	O	E	R
O	R	E	E	P	O	E	R	J	F	J	R	E	G	L	R	J	P	L	T
O	S	N	T	U	L	R	E	Z	E	O	E	S	A	O	T	X	U	U	S
U	C	N	B	O	A	G	I	U	L	W	R	L	U	B	I	A	O	H	G
R	Q	I	A	T	S	R	G	P	I	M	W	O	L	R	P	H	L	N	O
T	T	S	T	S	O	K	T	A	O	A	A	Z	V	T	O	H	E	A	S
H	C	I	O	O	N	U	P	A	E	T	S	B	E	L	F	Y	O	V	K
O	H	V	C	M	A	N	H	K	T	O	H	D	W	P	G	I	M	N	M
U	A	E	R	O	W	O	T	E	R	E	R	R	I	Z	B	E	O	O	A
S	L	V	L	R	A	I	L	W	A	Y	O	I	Y	D	G	D	L	H	R
E	G	U	P	E	R	Z	I	N	E	Y	W	V	Z	I	Z	F	K	O	K
O	W	A	X	W	O	R	K	O	O	P	L	E	R	O	W	N	E	N	W
N	U	F	O	R	E	U	O	N	E	T	O	R	C	A	N	N	O	T	I

Without	Upperclassman	Courthouse	Lifelike	Washbowl
Cabdriver	Butterscotch	Uprising	Teaspoon	Handmade

Spelling Test

Your Answers		Correct Spelling If Incorrect	
1	_____	1	_____
2	_____	2	_____
3	_____	3	_____
4	_____	4	_____
5	_____	5	_____
6	_____	6	_____
7	_____	7	_____
8	_____	8	_____
9	_____	9	_____
10	_____	10	_____
11	_____	11	_____
12	_____	12	_____
13	_____	13	_____
14	_____	14	_____
15	_____	15	_____
16	_____	16	_____
17	_____	17	_____
18	_____	18	_____
19	_____	19	_____
20	_____	20	_____

Class: _____

		Week:				Week:				Week:				Week:			
Day		M	T	W	Th	F	M	T	W	Th	F	M	T	W	Th	F	M	T	W	Th	F
Date																					
Assignments																					

(grade rows numbered 1–32)

This book list commonly misspelled words that get butchered daily. You should test your child on these words at the start of the school year to determine which words require additional focus. Test your child again mid-year and at the end of the year to monitor progress.

Spelling Weekly Study Strategies

Monday - Take a pretest to determine which words the student needs to study.

Tuesday - Thursday - Study the new spelling words. Try different spelling activities like writing a definition or sentence for each word, write words on individual index cards to study, etc.

Friday - Retest to determine which words were mastered. (There are some blank testing sheets in the back of this book.)

Depending on your location some words might not be so common to you but, they are common in other areas and to someone else. This gives the student a chance to learn new words.

Name _____

Date _____

Common Misspelled Words Practice

Spell each of your words by looking carefully at the spelling, covering the word up and then try writing it by yourself.

A lot	Awhile	About	Absence	Academic
Accept	Access	Accidentally	Accompanying	Accomplish
Accomplishment	According	Accordion	Accurate	Accuse
Ache	Acquaint	Acquaintance	Acquire	Across
Activities	Actual	Adapt	Address	Adjacent

Name _____

Date _____

Common Misspelled Words Practice

Spell each of your words by looking carefully at the spelling, covering the word up and then try writing it by yourself.

Adolescent	Adopt	Advantageous	Adverse	Advertisement
Advice	Advise	Affect	Again	Aggravate
Aisle	AllReady	All Right	All Together	Allot
Allude	Allusion	Almost	Along	Alphabet
Already	Alright	Alter	Although	Altogether

Name _____

Date _____

Common Misspelled Words Practice

Spell each of your words by looking carefully at the spelling, covering the word up and then try writing it by yourself.

Always	Amateur	Among	Amount	Analysis

Analyze	Answer	Antidote	Antiseptic	Anxiety

Anxious	Anyplace	Anywhere	Apartment	Apology

Apparently	Appearance	Applied	Approach	Appropriate

April	Arctic	Argue	Argument	Arithmetic

Name _____

Date _____

Common Misspelled Words Practice

Spell each of your words by looking carefully at the spelling, covering the word up and then try writing it by yourself.

Aroused	Artic	Article	Ascend	Assure
Athletic	Athletics	Attack	Attendance	Attitude
Audience	Aunt	Author	Autumn	Auxiliary
Averse	Awful	Awfully	Awhile	Awkward
Bachelor	Bad	Badly	Balloon	Barbecue

Name _____

Date _____

Common Misspelled Words Practice

Spell each of your words by looking carefully at the spelling, covering the word up and then try writing it by yourself.

Basically	Basis	Beautiful	Because	Because Of
Becoming	Been	Before	Beginning	Belief
Believe	Believing	Beneficial	Beside	Besides
Between	Birthday	Biscuit	Blue	Bought
Breath	Breathe	Built	Business	Busy

Name _____

Date _____

Common Misspelled Words Practice

Spell each of your words by looking carefully at the spelling, covering the word up and then try writing it by yourself.

Cafeteria	Calendar	Campaign	Capital	Capitol
Carrying	Celebrate	Cemetery	Censor	Censure
Challenge	Changeable	Changing	Characteristic	Chauffeur
Cheerfulness	Chief	Children	Chocolate	Choose
Chose	Chosen	Christmas	Cite	Claus

Name _____

Date _____

Common Misspelled Words Practice

Spell each of your words by looking carefully at the spelling, covering the word up and then try writing it by yourself.

Climbed	Close	Cloth	Clothes	Clothing
Coincidence	Color	Column	Come	Comfortably
Coming	Committee	Companies	Compare To	Compare With
Compel	Competence	Complement	Compliment	Comprehension
Concede	Conceive	Concern	Condemn	Congratulations

Name _____

Date _____

Common Misspelled Words Practice

Spell each of your words by looking carefully at the spelling, covering the word up and then try writing it by yourself.

Connoisseur	Conscience	Conscious	Considerable	Consistent
Contemporary	Contempt	Continual	Continuous	Controlled
Convenience	Correspondence	Cough	CouldHave	Council
Councilor	Counsel	Counselor	Country	Courageous
Cousin	Criticism	Cupboard	Curiosity	Curriculum

Name _____

Date _____

Common Misspelled Words Practice

Spell each of your words by looking carefully at the spelling, covering the word up and then try writing it by yourself.

Cylinder	Daily	Dairy	Dangerous	Dear

Deceive	Decidedly	Decorate	Deficient	Definite

Delinquent	Democracy	Dependent	Descendant	Descent

Describe	Desert	Design	Despair	Dessert

Detriment	Develop	Device	Devices	Devise

Name _____

Date _____

Common Misspelled Words Practice

Spell each of your words by looking carefully at the spelling, covering the word up and then try writing it by yourself.

Dictionary	Difference	Different From	Different Than	Dilemma

Diminish	Dining Room	Disappoint	Disastrous	Disciple

Discoveries	Discuss	Disease	Disinterested	Dissatisfied

Distinguished	Doctor	Does	Dominant	Dormitories

Drunkenness	Due To	Eager	Early	Easily

Name _____

Date _____

Common Misspelled Words Practice

Spell each of your words by looking carefully at the spelling, covering the word up and then try writing it by yourself.

Easter	Easy	Ecstasy	Edition	Effect
Efficient	Eighth	Either	Eligible	Eloquently
Elude	Embarrass	Emigrate	Emphasize	Emptiness
Enemies	Enemy	Enormous	Enough	Ensure
Enthusiasm	Environment	Equally	Equipped	Escape

Name _____

Date _____

Common Misspelled Words Practice

Spell each of your words by looking carefully at the spelling, covering the word up and then try writing it by yourself.

Especially	Eventually	Every	Every Day	Every One

Everybody	Everyday	Everyone	Exaggerating	Exceed

Except	Excess	Exercise	Exhausted	Exhibit

Exhilarate	Existence	Existent	Expect	Extravagant

Facilities	Faithfulness	Familiar	Families	Farther

Name _____

Date _____

Common Misspelled Words Practice

Spell each of your words by looking carefully at the spelling,
covering the word up and then try writing it by yourself.

Fascinating	Favorite	Feasible	February	Fictitious
Fierce	Financially	First	Football	Foreign
Foreword	Formally	Former	Formerly	Forty
Forward	Fourteen	Fourth	Friday	Friend
Fuel	Fulfill	Funeral	Further	Gaiety

Common Misspelled Words Practice

Spell each of your words by looking carefully at the spelling, covering the word up and then try writing it by yourself.

Gauge	Generally	Genius	Genuine	Getting
Goes	Goggles	Government	Grade	Grammar
Grandeur	Grievous	Guarantee	Guard	Guess
Half	Halloween	Handicapped	Handkerchief	Hanged
Happening	Happily	Harass	Haughtiness	Having

Name _____

Date _____

Common Misspelled Words Practice

Spell each of your words by looking carefully at the spelling, covering the word up and then try writing it by yourself.

Healthful	Healthy	Hear	Heard	Heavier
Height	Hello	Helpful	Here	Hindrance
Hoarse	Hoping	Hopping	Hospital	Hour
House	However	Huge	Humiliate	Hung
Hurriedly	Hygiene	Hypocrite	Ideally	Ignorance

Name _____

Date _____

Common Misspelled Words Practice

Spell each of your words by looking carefully at the spelling, covering the word up and then try writing it by yourself.

Illusion	Imaginary	Immediately	Immense	Imply
Important	Inadequate	Inauguration	Increase	Incredible
Indictment	Indispensable	Individual	Infer	Influence
Ingenious	Initiative	Innocence	Insistence	Instead
Instructor	Insure	Intellectual	Intelligent	Interest

Name _____

Date _____

Common Misspelled Words Practice

Spell each of your words by looking carefully at the spelling, covering the word up and then try writing it by yourself.

Interpretation	Intolerance	Introductory	Invariable	Irrelevant
Irresistible	Island	Its	January	Jealously
Jealousy	Jewelry	Kindergarten	Knew	Know
Knowledge	Labeled	Laboratory	Laid	Language
Later	Latter	Lead	Led	Leisurely

Name _____

Date _____

Common Misspelled Words Practice

Spell each of your words by looking carefully at the spelling, covering the word up and then try writing it by yourself.

Lengthening	Lessons	Letter	License	Lieutenant

Lightening	Lightning	Little	Liveliest	Loneliness

Loose	Lose	Loving	Loyalty	Luxuries

Magazine	Magnificent	Maintenance	Making	Maneuver

Manufacturing	Many	Marriage	Mathematics	MayBe

Name

Date

Common Misspelled Words Practice

Spell each of your words by looking carefully at the spelling, covering the word up and then try writing it by yourself.

Maybe	Meant	Mechanics	Medicine	Metropolitan
Miniature	Minute	Minutes	Miscellaneous	Mischief
Misspelled	Monotonous	Moral	Morale	Morning
Mosquitoes	Mother	Much	Multiplication	Muscle
Must Have	Mysterious	Name	Naturally	Nausea

Name _____

Date _____

Common Misspelled Words Practice

Spell each of your words by looking carefully at the spelling, covering the word up and then try writing it by yourself.

Nauseated	Nauseating	Nauseous	Necessary	Neglect
Negation	Neighbor	Neither	Nice	Niece
Ninety	Ninth	None	Noticeable	Noticing
Number	Numerous	Obedience	Obstacle	Occasion
Occur	Occurred	Occurrence	Off	Offered

Name _____

Date _____

Common Misspelled Words Practice

Spell each of your words by looking carefully at the spelling, covering the word up and then try writing it by yourself.

Often	Omit	Omitted	Once	Opinion
Opportunities	Oppose	Optimism	Optimistic	Origin
Outside	Overwhelming	Pamphlet	Pandemonium	Pantomime
Parallel	Paralyze	Particularly	Party	Passed
Past	Peace	Peculiar	Peculiarities	People

Name _____

Date _____

Common Misspelled Words Practice

Spell each of your words by looking carefully at the spelling, covering the word up and then try writing it by yourself.

Perceive	Performance	Permanent	Permit	Persistent
Personal	Personnel	Perspective	Perspiration	Persuade
Phase	Phenomenon	Philosophy	Physical	Picnicking
Piece	Planned	Planning	Played	Plays
Playwright	Please	Poison	Politician	Politics

Name _____

Date _____

Common Misspelled Words Practice

Spell each of your words by looking carefully at the spelling, covering the word up and then try writing it by yourself.

Portrayed	Possess	Possessions	Possible	Practically

Practice	Prairie	Precede	Precedent	Prefer

Preferred	Prejudice	Prepare	Prescription	Presence

Pretty	Previous	Primitive	Principal	Principle

Privilege	Probably	Procedure	Proceed	Pronounce

Name _____

Date _____

Common Misspelled Words Practice

Spell each of your words by looking carefully at the spelling, covering the word up and then try writing it by yourself.

Proprietor	Prospective	Psychology	Punctuation	Qualities
Quarter	Questionnaire	Quiet	Quit	Quite
Quizzes	Quotation	Quote	Raise	Read
Real	Realize	Really	Receive	Received
Recognize	Recommend	Reference	Referred	Referring

Name _____

Date _____

Common Misspelled Words Practice

Spell each of your words by looking carefully at the spelling,
covering the word up and then try writing it by yourself.

Regrettable	Relief	Relieve	Religion	Remember
Reminisce	Renowned	Repetition	Representative	Research
Resemble	Resources	Restaurant	Reverence	Reverend
Rhythm	Ridiculous	Right	Righteous	Rivalry
Rough	Route	Safety	Said	Sandwich

Name _____

Date _____

Common Misspelled Words Practice

Spell each of your words by looking carefully at the spelling, covering the word up and then try writing it by yourself.

Santa	Satisfaction	Saturday	Saucer	Says
Scarcity	Scene	Schedule	Scheme	Scholarship
School	Schoolhouse	Scientific	Secretary	Seize
Sentence	Separate	Several	Shepherd	Shining
Shoes	Shoulder	Shriek	Siege	Sight

Name _____

Date _____

Common Misspelled Words Practice

Spell each of your words by looking carefully at the spelling, covering the word up and then try writing it by yourself.

Significance	Similar	Since	Sincerely	Site
Skiing	Skis	Sole	Some	Some time
Something	Sometime	Sometimes	Soon	Sophomore
Sorrowful	Soul	Sovereignty	Specially	Specifically
Specimen	Sponsor	Stationary	Stationery	Stenographer

Common Misspelled Words Practice

Spell each of your words by looking carefully at the spelling, covering the word up and then try writing it by yourself.

Stopping	Store	Straight	Straighten	Strength
Strenuous	Stubborn	Studying	Substantiate	Subtle
Succeed	Succeeding	Successful	Suddenness	Sufficient
Sugar	Summary	Summer	Sunday	Supersede
Supervisor	Suppose	Supposed To	Sure	Surely

Name _____

Date _____

Common Misspelled Words Practice

Spell each of your words by looking carefully at the spelling, covering the word up and then try writing it by yourself.

Surprise	Surrounded	Susceptible	Suspense	Suspicious
Swimming	Syllable	Symmetrical	Synonymous	Teacher
Tear	Technical	Technique	Temperature	Temporarily
Tenant	Tenement	Terrible	Than	Thanksgiving
That	Their	Then	Theories	There

Common Misspelled Words Practice

Spell each of your words by looking carefully at the spelling, covering the word up and then try writing it by yourself.

Therefore	They	Thirtieth	Thorough	Thoroughly
Though	Thought	Through	Till	Tired
To	Together	Tomorrow	Tonight	Too
Toys	Tragedy	Train	Transferred	Traveling
Tremendous	Trespass	Trouble	Truly	Tuesday

Name _____

Date _____

Common Misspelled Words Practice

Spell each of your words by looking carefully at the spelling, covering the word up and then try writing it by yourself.

Twelfth	Two	Typical	Tyranny	Unbelievable
Unconscious	Undesirable	Undoubtedly	Uneasiness	Unforgettable
Uninterested	Unique	Unmanageable	Unnecessary	Until
Usage	Use	Used	Used to	Useful
Usual	Usually	Vacation	Vacuum	Valleys

Name

Date

Common Misspelled Words Practice

Spell each of your words by looking carefully at the spelling, covering the word up and then try writing it by yourself.

Valuable	Varieties	Vaudeville	Vegetable	Vengeance
Ventilate	Very	Veteran	Vicinity	Victim
View	Village	Villain	Vinegar	Visible
Visitor	Vitamin	Volume	Waive	Wave
Wealthiest	Wear	Weather	Wednesday	Weigh

Name _____

Date _____

Common Misspelled Words Practice

Spell each of your words by looking carefully at the spelling,
covering the word up and then try writing it by yourself.

Weird	Were	Whenever	Where	Wherever
Whether	Which	White	Who	Whole
Wholly	Whose	Witnessed	Women	Wonderful
Wrench	Write	Writing	Wrote	Yacht
Yield	Your	Yours	Zenith	Zinc

Commonly misspelled words that sound alike but are spelled differently

Carefully circle the correct spelling combinations of words.

	A	B	C	D
1.	Abal/Able	Abell/Able	Aball/Able	Abel/Able
2.	Accede/Exceed	Accede/Excead	Acede/Excead	Acede/Exceed
3.	Acsept/Except	Acept/Except	Asept/Except	Accept/Except
4.	Acts/Ax	Actts/sx	Actl/Ax	Actts/Ax
5.	AdyAdd	Ad/Ad	Ad/Add	Ad/An
6.	Adam/Attum	Adam/Attom	Adam/Atom	Adam/Atum
7.	Additoin/Edition	Adition/Edition	Aditoin/Edition	Addition/Edition
8.	Adieo/Ado	Adeio/Ado	Adeiu/Ado	Adieu/Ado
9.	Aerrial/Areil	Aerrial/Ariel	Aerial/Areil	Aerial/Ariel
10.	Aphfect/Effect	Afect/Effect	Aphect/Effect	Affect/Effect
11.	Aphfected/Effected	Aphected/Effected	Afected/Effected	Affected/Effected
12.	Aphfects/Effects	Afects/Effects	Affects/Effects	Aphects/Effects
13.	Afterward/Afterword	Aphterward/Afterword	Aphfterward/Afterword	Affterward/Afterword
14.	Aid/Aide	Aad/Aide	Aid/Aie	Aid/Aei
15.	Aall/Ale	Aill/Ale	Ail/Ale	Aal/Ale
16.	Air/Heir/Er	Air/Hier/Err	Air/Hier/Er	Air/Heir/Err
17.	Aasle/Isle/I'll	Aisle/Isle/I'll	Aisle/Isle/I'l	Aasle/Isle/I'l
18.	Alle/Aal	Ale/Aal	Alle/Ail	Ale/Ail
19.	Al Ways/Always	Al Weys/Always	All Weys/Always	All Ways/Always
20.	All/Awl	All/Aml	Al/Awp	Al/Awl
21.	Allowed/Alood	Allowed/Aloud	Alowed/Aloud	Alowed/Alood

Commonly misspelled words that sound alike but are spelled differently

Carefully circle the correct spelling combinations of words.

	A	B	C	D
1.	Suite/Sweat	Suite/Swet	Suite/Sweet	Soite/Swet
2.	Tame/Thyme	Time/Thye	Time/Thyme	Tame/Thye
3.	Inttence/Intents	Intence/Intents	Intense/Intents	Inttense/Intents
4.	Packed/Pactt	Packed/Pact	Paked/Pactt	Paked/Pact
5.	Allode/Elude	Alude/Elude	Allude/Elude	Alode/Elude
6.	Rheum/Rom	Rheom/Rom	Rheum/Room	Rheum/Roum
7.	Rowed/Road	Ruwed/Rod	Rowed/Rod	Ruwed/Road
8.	Duel/Dual	Duell/Dual	Duel/Daul	Duell/Daul
9.	Chote/Shot	Chute/Shoot	Chute/Shout	Chute/Shot
10.	Mist/Missed	Mist/Mised	Mist/Misced	Mist/Miced
11.	Feintt/Faint	Fientt/Faint	Feint/Faint	Fient/Faint
12.	Faon/Fawn	Faun/Fawn	Faun/Faw	Fuan/Fawn
13.	Frryer/Frair	Fryer/Friar	Fryer/Frair	Frryer/Friar
14.	Arrk/Arc	Arrck/Arc	Ark/Arc	Arck/Arc
15.	Ilacit/Elicit	Illicit/Elicit	Ilicit/Elicit	Illacit/Elicit
16.	Yaw/Ewe	Yew/Ewe	Yew/Ee	Yaw/Ee
17.	Tead/Tide	Tied/Tide	Teid/Tide	Taed/Tide
18.	Forrth/Foorth	Forrth/Fourth	Forth/Fourth	Forth/Foorth
19.	Morrning/Mourning	Morning/Moorning	Morrning/Moorning	Morning/Mourning
20.	Rutte/Wrote	Rute/Wrote	Rote/Wrote	Rotte/Wrote

Commonly misspelled words that sound alike but are spelled differently

Carefully circle the correct spelling combinations of words.

	A	B	C	D
1.	Mourrn/Morn	Moorrn/Morn	Mourn/Morn	Moorn/Morn
2.	Bech/Beach	Beech/Beach	Beech/Baech	Bech/Baech
3.	Byte/Bight/Bite	Byte/Baght/Bite	Bytte/Baght/Bite	Bytte/Bight/Bite
4.	Dye/Dae	Dye/Die	Dye/Dea	Dye/Dei
5.	Sane/Seine	Sane/Seane	Sane/Siene	Sane/Saene
6.	Brraek/Brake	Break/Brake	Brreak/Brake	Braek/Brake
7.	Fare/Fair	Farre/Fiar	Farre/Fair	Fare/Fiar
8.	Yourr/You're	Yoor/You're	Yoorr/You're	Your/You're
9.	Broach/Broch	Bruach/Broch	Broach/Brouch	Broach/Brooch
10.	Brred/Bread	Bred/Bread	Brred/Braed	Bred/Braed
11.	Czech/Check	Czech/Chek	Czech/Chek	Czech/Chec
12.	Reel/Rael	Reel/Real	Rel/Rael	Rel/Real
13.	Accede/Excead	Acede/Exceed	Accede/Exceed	Acede/Excead
14.	Fllue/Flow	Flloe/Flow	Flue/Flow	Floe/Flow
15.	Fourrth/Forth	Foorth/Forth	Fourth/Forth	Foorrth/Forth
16.	Gillt/Guilt	Gilt/Goilt	Gilt/Guilt	Gillt/Goilt
17.	Aerial/Areil	Aerrial/Ariel	Aerrial/Areil	Aerial/Ariel
18.	Beao/Bow	Beau/Bow	Baeu/Bow	Baeo/Bow
19.	Tigress/Tigris	Tigresc/Tigris	Tigres/Tigris	Tagres/Tigris
20.	Whales/Wials/Wales	Whales/Wails/Wales	Whalles/Wails/Wales	Whalles/Wials/Wales

Commonly misspelled words that sound alike but are spelled differently

Carefully circle the correct spelling combinations of words.

	A	B	C	D
1.	Herd/Heard	Herrd/Haerd	Herrd/Heard	Herd/Haerd
2.	Idle/Idol/Idyl	Idle/Idul/Idyll	Idle/Idol/Idyll	Idle/Idul/Idyl
3.	Toul/Tulle	Tool/Tulle	Tol/Tulle	Tol/Tolle
4.	Cypres/Cyprus	Cypresc/Cyprus	Cypres/Cypros	Cypress/Cyprus
5.	Knightt/Night	Knaghtt/Night	Knight/Night	Knaght/Night
6.	Berrth/Barth	Berth/Barth	Berth/Birth	Berrth/Birth
7.	Ax/Actss	Ax/Acts	AxhActs	Ax/Actts
8.	Huld/Holed	Holld/Holed	Hold/Holed	Hulld/Holed
9.	Oral/Aoral	Oral/Aural	Orral/Aural	Orral/Aoral
10.	Exerrcice/Exorcise	Exercise/Exorcise	Exercice/Exorcise	Exerrcise/Exorcise
11.	Neise/Nice	Niese/Nice	Niece/Nice	Neice/Nice
12.	Leassed/Least	Leased/Least	Laessed/Least	Laesed/Least
13.	Crraft/Kraft	Craft/Kraft	Crrapht/Kraft	Crapht/Kraft
14.	Taked/Tactt	Taked/Tact	Tacked/Tactt	Tacked/Tact
15.	Chence/Chantts	Chance/Chantts	Chence/Chants	Chance/Chants
16.	Miry/Marry/Merry	Mary/Marry/Merry	Mary/Mary/Merry	Miry/Mary/Merry
17.	Ducksc/Ducts	Ducks/Ducts	Duks/Ducts	Duckss/Ducts
18.	Faze/Phase	Faze/Phasce	Faze/Phasse	Faze/Phace
19.	Bascil/Basal	Basal/Basal	Bassil/Basal	Basil/Basal

Commonly misspelled words that sound alike but are spelled differently

Carefully circle the correct spelling combinations of words.

	A	B	C	D
1.	Waek/Wek	Waek/Week	Weak/Week	Weak/Wek
2.	Ball/Bawl	Bill/Bawl	Bal/Bawl	Bil/Bawl
3.	Teem/Team	Tem/Team	Teem/Taem	Tem/Taem
4.	Lea/Lay	Lei/Lay	Lae/Lay	Lie/Lay
5.	Knit/Nit	Knat/Nit	Knitt/Nit	Knatt/Nit
6.	Sacks/Sax	Saks/Sax	Sackss/Sax	Sacksc/Sax
7.	Summary/Summery	Sommary/Summery	Sumary/Summery	Somary/Summery
8.	Marc/Mark	Marrc/Mark	Marc/Marck	Marrc/Marck
9.	Mary/Merry/Mary	Mirry/Merry/Mary	Miry/Merry/Mary	Marry/Merry/Mary
10.	Jim/Jamb	Jim/Jab	Jam/Jab	Jam/Jamb
11.	Wek/Waek	Week/Waek	Week/Weak	Wek/Weak
12.	Walles/Whales/Wials	Wales/Whales/Wails	Wales/Whales/Wials	Walles/Whales/Wails
13.	Romer/Rumor	Roumer/Rumor	Roomer/Rumor	Romer/Romor
14.	Waills/Wales/Whales	Wails/Wales/Whales	Wialls/Wales/Whales	Wials/Wales/Whales
15.	Nive/Knave	Nave/Knave	Nave/Knea	Nave/Knae
16.	Fleir/Flyer	Fllier/Flyer	Flleir/Flyer	Flier/Flyer
17.	Wet/Whet	Wett/Whet	Watt/Whet	Wat/Whet
18.	Chord/Cord	Churrd/Cord	Chorrd/Cord	Churd/Cord
19.	Cesion/Session	Cession/Session	Cessoin/Session	Cesoin/Session
20.	Knot/Not	Knutt/Not	Knut/Not	Knott/Not
21.	Weighed/Wade	Wieghed/Wade	Weaghed/Wade	Waeghed/Wade
22.	Merry/Miry/Marry	Merry/Mary/Marry	Mery/Mary/Marry	Mery/Miry/Marry

#			
23.	Tie/Thai	Tei/Thai	Tae/Thai	Tea/Thai
24.	Waiter/Wader	Waitter/Wader	Wiatter/Wader	Wiater/Wader
25.	Know/o	Know/No	Knuw/o	Knuw/No
26.	Massed/Mast	Masced/Mast	Mased/Mast	Maced/Mast
27.	Herrtz/Horts	Herrtz/Hurts	Hertz/Hurts	Hertz/Horts
28.	Thiers/There's	Theirrs/There's	Thierrs/There's	Theirs/There's
29.	Metteor/Meateir	Meteor/Meateir	Meteor/Meatier	Metteor/Meatier
30.	Ham/Hymn	Ham/Hyn	Him/Hymn	Him/Hyn
31.	Batted/Baited	Batted/Biated	Bated/Biated	Bated/Baited
32.	Chauffeur/Shofar	Chuaffeur/Shofar	Chuafeur/Shofar	Chaufeur/Shofar
33.	Jibe/Gie	Jibe/Gei	Jabe/Gibe	Jibe/Gibe
34.	Hue/Hugh/Hew	Hoe/Hugh/Hw	Hue/Hugh/Hw	Hoe/Hugh/Hew
35.	Roosse	Rowse	Rouse	Rousse
36.	Rek/Wreak	Rek/Wraek	Reek/Wreak	Reek/Wraek
37.	Moorrning/Morning	Moorning/Morning	Mourning/Morning	Mourrning/Morning
38.	Here/Hear	Herre/Hear	Herre/Haer	Here/Haer
39.	Coorrse/Coarse	Course/Coarse	Courrse/Coarse	Coorse/Coarse
40.	Whine/Wine	Whine/Wie	Whane/Wine	Whine/Wei
41.	Lade/Laad	Lade/Liad	Lide/Laad	Lade/Laid
42.	Led/Leid	Led/Laed	Led/Lied	Led/Lead
43.	Biat/Bate	Biatt/Bate	Bait/Bate	Baitt/Bate
44.	Foaled/Fold	Foalled/Fold	Fualed/Fold	Fualled/Fold
45.	Oh/Owa	Oh/Oa	Oh/Oe	Oh/Owe
46.	We'l/Wheal	We'l/Wheel	We'll/Wheel	We'll/Wheal
47.	Ewes/Yews/Use	Ewesc/Yews/Use	Ewess/Yews/Use	Ewes/Yews/Uce
48.	You'Re/Yore/Your	You'Re/Yorre/Your	Yoo'Re/Yore/Your	Yoo'Re/Yorre/Your
49.	Flair/Flare	Fliar/Flare	Flliar/Flare	Fllair/Flare
50.	Bured/Bird	Borred/Bird	Bored/Bird	Burred/Bird
51.	Raise/Reys/Raze	Raise/Rays/Raze	Raisse/Rays/Raze	Raisse/Reys/Raze

52.	Maul/Mall	Mual/Mal	Maul/Mal	Mual/Mall
53.	Bale/Bal/Bail	Bale/Bal/Bial	Bale/Baal/Bial	Bale/Baal/Bail
54.	Sttatoinary/Stationery	Stationary/Stationery	Statoinary/Stationery	Sttationary/Stationery
55.	Fairy/Fery	Fiary/Fery	Fairy/Ferry	Fiary/Ferry
56.	Lapps/Laps/Lapse	Lapps/Laps/Lapce	Laps/Laps/Lapce	Laps/Laps/Lapse
57.	Chassed/Chaste	Chased/Chaste	Chasced/Chaste	Chaced/Chaste
58.	Chiorr/Quire	Chior/Quire	Choirr/Quire	Choir/Quire
59.	Baron/Baren	Baron/Barren	Barun/Barren	Barun/Baren
60.	Crrape/Crepe	Crripe/Crepe	Crape/Crepe	Cripe/Crepe
61.	Cllik/Clique	Cllick/Clique	Click/Clique	Clik/Clique
62.	Whett/Wet	Whet/Wet	Whatt/Wet	What/Wet
63.	Lama/Llama	Lima/Llama	Lama/Lllama	Lima/Lllama
64.	Toad/Toed/Towd	Tuad/Toed/Towd	Tuad/Toed/Towed	Toad/Toed/Towed
65.	Crruel/Crewel	Crroel/Crewel	Croel/Crewel	Cruel/Crewel
66.	Lean/Lien	Lean/Lean	Lean/Laen	Lean/Lein
67.	Muscle/Mussel	Muscle/Musel	Mussle/Musel	Mussle/Mussel
68.	Flew/Flu/Flue	Fllew/Flu/Flue	Flew/Flo/Flue	Fllew/Flo/Flue
69.	Foe/Fuax	Fue/Faox	Foe/Faux	Foe/Faox
70.	Mane/Maane/Main	Mane/Miane/Main	Mane/Maine/Main	Mane/Maane/Mian
71.	Sttraight/Strait	Straight/Strait	Sttriaght/Strait	Striaght/Strait
72.	Lax/Lacksc	Lax/Laks	Lax/Lackss	Lax/Lacks
73.	Faancé/Faincée	Faincé/Fiancée	Fiancé/Fiancée	Faancé/Fiancée
74.	Tacks/Tax	Tacksc/Tax	Tackss/Tax	Taks/Tax
75.	Mewsc/Muse	Mewss/Muse	Mews/Muce	Mews/Muse
76.	Wholly/Holay/Holy	Wholly/Holey/Holy	Wholy/Holay/Holy	Wholy/Holey/Holy
77.	Wrast/Rest	Wrrest/Rest	Wrrast/Rest	Wrest/Rest
78.	Hurrde/Hoard	Horrde/Hoard	Hurde/Hoard	Horde/Hoard
79.	Rode/Rud	Rode/Rued	Rude/Rued	Rude/Rud
80.	Raed/Red	Ried/Red	Reid/Red	Read/Red

81.	Wok/Walk	Wock/Wallk	Wock/Walk	Wok/Wallk
82.	Mein/Mean	Mean/Mean	Maen/Mean	Mien/Mean
83.	Throws/Throes	Thruws/Throes	Thrrows/Throes	Thrruws/Throes
84.	Hue/Ho	Hoe/Ho	Hue/o	Hoe/o
85.	Swet/Suite	Sweet/Suite	Swet/Soite	Sweat/Suite
86.	Wrute/Rote	Wrrute/Rote	Wrrote/Rote	Wrote/Rote
87.	Overdo/Overdue	Overrdo/Overdoe	Overdo/Overdoe	Overrdo/Overdue
88.	Red/Read	Red/Reid	Red/Ried	Red/Raed
89.	Sac/Sak	Sac/Sak	Sac/Sac	Sac/Sack
90.	Peaan/Paeun	Peaan/Paeon	Paean/Paeon	Paean/Paeun
91.	He'Ll/Hael/Hel	He'Ll/Heal/Hel	He'Ll/Hael/Heel	He'Ll/Heal/Heel
92.	Ad/Ax	Ad/Add	Ad/Agd	Ad/Ad
93.	Oversaes/Oversees	Oversaes/Overses	Overseas/Overses	Overseas/Oversees
94.	Imanent/Imminent	Immanent/Immanent	Immanent/Imminent	Imanent/Immanent
95.	Hymn/Him	Hymn/Ham	Hymn/Ha	Hymn/Hi
96.	Handssome/Hansom	Handscome/Hansom	Handsome/Hansom	Handsume/Hansom
97.	Karat/Carat/Carrot/Caret	Karat/Carat/Carot/Caret	Karat/Carat/Carrut/Caret	Karat/Carat/Carut/Caret
98.	Wood/Woold	Wood/Would	Wod/Woold	Wod/Would
99.	Crewel/Cruel	Crrewel/Croel	Crrewel/Cruel	Crewel/Croel
100.	Canun/Canon	Canon/Canon	Cannun/Canon	Cannon/Canon
101.	Find/Fined	Fand/Fined	Find/Find	Fand/Find
102.	Grasly/Grizly	Grasly/Grizzly	Grisly/Grizzly	Grisly/Grizly
103.	Jal/Gel	Jall/Gel	Jell/Gel	Jel/Gel
104.	Lane/Lian	Lane/Laan	Line/Laan	Lane/Lain
105.	Cerael/Serial	Cerreal/Serial	Cereal/Serial	Cerrael/Serial
106.	Saverr/Savur	Saverr/Savor	Saver/Savor	Saver/Savur
107.	Ducts/Ducks	Ducts/Duks	Ductts/Ducks	Ductts/Duks
108.	Rigor/Riger	Rigor/Rijer	Rigor/Rigjer	Rigor/Rigger
109.	Waned/Whined/Wind	Wined/Whined/Wid	Waned/Whined/Wid	Wined/Whined/Wind

110.	Whey/Way/Waegh	Whey/Way/Weagh	Whey/Way/Weigh	Whey/Way/Wiegh
111.	Foreword/Forward	Furreword/Forward	Forreword/Forward	Fureword/Forward
112.	Flocks/Phlox	Flloks/Phlox	Floks/Phlox	Fllocks/Phlox
113.	Retch/Wretch	Ratch/Wretch	Rattch/Wretch	Rettch/Wretch
114.	There/They'Re/Their	Therre/They'Re/Thier	There/They'Re/Thier	Therre/They'Re/Their
115.	Mute/Moat	Mutte/Moat	Mote/Moat	Motte/Moat
116.	Tee/Tae	Te/Tea	Tee/Tea	Te/Tae
117.	Moose/Moosse	Mose/Mousse	Moose/Mousse	Mose/Moosse
118.	Tic/Tick	Tic/Tik	Tic/Tik	Tic/Tic
119.	Metal	Metil	Mettil	Mettal
120.	Meet/Mete/Meat	Meet/Mete/Maet	Met/Mete/Maet	Met/Mete/Meat
121.	Cated/Sided	Citted/Sided	Catted/Sided	Cited/Sided
122.	Hier/Er/Air	Hier/Err/Air	Heir/Err/Air	Heir/Er/Air
123.	Chews/Chose	Chews/Choose	Chews/Choos	Chews/Chouse
124.	Medal/Metal/Mettle/	Medal/Metal/Metle/	Medil/Metal/Mettle/	Medil/Metal/Metle/
125.	Flae/Flee	Flea/Fle	Flea/Flee	Flae/Fle
126.	Cousin/Cozen	Coosin/Cozen	Coussin/Cozen	Coossin/Cozen
127.	Gruan/Grown	Grroan/Grown	Groan/Grown	Grruan/Grown
128.	Teirr/Tear	Teir/Tear	Tier/Tear	Tierr/Tear
129.	Tactt/Tacked	Tact/Tacked	Tactt/Taked	Tact/Taked
130.	Cymball/Symbul	Cymbal/Symbul	Cymbal/Symbol	Cymball/Symbol
131.	Bullion/Bouillon	Buloin/Bouillon	Bulloin/Bouillon	Bulion/Bouillon
132.	Knew/New/Gno	Knew/New/Gnu	Knew/New/Go	Knew/New/Gu
133.	Brewed/Brood	Brewed/Brud	Brewed/Broud	Brewed/Brod
134.	Wain/Wane/Wayne	Waan/Wane/Wayne	Wain/Wane/Weyne	Waan/Wane/Weyne
135.	Nome/Gnoe	Nume/Gnome	Nome/Gnome	Nume/Gnoe
136.	Flyer/Fleir	Fllyer/Fleir	Fllyer/Flier	Flyer/Flier
137.	I/Aya/Eye	I/Aye/Ee	I/Aya/Ee	I/Aye/Eye
138.	Fowll/Fool	Fowl/Fool	Fowll/Foul	Fowl/Foul

139.	Isclet/Eyelet	Islat/Eyelet	Isslet/Eyelet	Islet/Eyelet
140.	Gild/Goild	Gild/Guild	Gilld/Goild	Gilld/Guild
141.	Asept/Except	Accept/Except	Acept/Except	Acsept/Except
142.	Cirrat/Karat	Carrat/Karat	Cirat/Karat	Carat/Karat
143.	Adieu/Ado	Adieo/Ado	Adeiu/Ado	Adeio/Ado
144.	Aphfect/Effect	Affect/Effect	Aphect/Effect	Afect/Effect
145.	Teas/Tease/Tes	Taes/Tease/Tes	Taes/Tease/Tees	Teas/Tease/Tees
146.	Ring/Wring	Rang/Wrring	Rang/Wring	Ring/Wrring
147.	Wiasst/Waste	Wiast/Waste	Waisst/Waste	Waist/Waste
148.	Brreys/Braise	Breys/Braise	Brays/Braise	Brrays/Braise
149.	Bery/Bory	Bery/Bury	Berry/Bury	Berry/Bory
150.	Tail/Tale	Taill/Tale	Tiall/Tale	Tial/Tale
151.	Mussed/Must	Mused/Must	Muced/Must	Musced/Must
152.	Pair/Pare/Paer	Pairr/Pare/Paer	Pairr/Pare/Pear	Pair/Pare/Pear
153.	Lae/Le	Lea/Lee	Lea/Le	Lae/Lee
154.	Roote/Rot	Route/Root	Route/Rot	Roote/Root
155.	Walk/Wok	Walck/Wok	Wallck/Wok	Wallk/Wok
156.	Medil	Medall	Medal	Medill
157.	Jinkss/Jinx	Jinks/Jinx	Jinksc/Jinx	Jincks/Jinx
158.	Terry/Tarry	Tery/Tarry	Tery/Tirry	Terry/Tirry
159.	Rays/Raze/Raise	Reys/Raze/Raise	Reyss/Raze/Raise	Rayss/Raze/Raise
160.	Wale/While	Wille/While	Wile/While	Walle/While
161.	Kraal/Crawl	Krial/Crawl	Kral/Crawl	Kril/Crawl
162.	Yews/Uce	Yewsc/Use	Yewss/Use	Yews/Use
163.	Lidder/Latter	Ladder/Latter	Lader/Latter	Lider/Latter
164.	Based/Baste	Bassed/Baste	Baced/Baste	Basced/Baste
165.	Wasste/Waist	Waste/Waist	Wasste/Wiast	Waste/Wiast
166.	Nice/Niece	Nise/Neice	Nise/Niece	Nice/Neice
167.	Root/Roote	Root/Route	Rot/Roote	Rot/Route

168.	Or/Ore/Oir	Orr/Ore/Oar	Or/Ore/Oar	Orr/Ore/Oir
169.	Hual/Hal	Hual/Hall	Haul/Hal	Haul/Hall
170.	Hart/Heart	Harrt/Haert	Harrt/Heart	Hart/Haert
171.	Thrrues/Throws	Throes/Throws	Thrroes/Throws	Thrues/Throws
172.	Hop/Whoup	Hoop/Whoop	Houp/Whoop	Hop/Whoop
173.	Inn/Ic	Inn/In	In/qn	In/In
174.	Eyallet/Islet	Eyellet/Islet	Eyalet/Islet	Eyelet/Islet
175.	Tes/Teas/Tease	Tees/Teas/Tease	Tes/Taes/Tease	Tees/Taes/Tease
176.	World/Whirled	Worrld/Whirled	Wurrld/Whirled	Wurld/Whirled
177.	Haerrd/Herd	Heard/Herd	Haerd/Herd	Hearrd/Herd
178.	Whaks/Wax	Whacks/Wax	Whackss/Wax	Whacksc/Wax
179.	Soe/Sioux	Soe/Soiux	Sue/Soiux	Sue/Sioux
180.	Graet/Grate	Grreat/Grate	Grraet/Grate	Great/Grate
181.	Bass/Base	Bas/Bace	Basc/Base	Bas/Base
182.	Fllu/Flue/Flew	Flu/Flue/Flew	Fllo/Flue/Flew	Flo/Flue/Flew
183.	Grrate/Graet	Grate/Great	Grrate/Great	Grate/Graet
184.	Innocence/Innocents	Innocance/Innocents	Inocence/Innocents	Inocance/Innocents
185.	Bal/Bial/Bale	Baal/Bial/Bale	Baal/Bail/Bale	Bal/Bail/Bale
186.	Wurd/Whirred	Word/Whired	Word/Whirred	Wurd/Whired
187.	Wayss/Weighs	Ways/Wieghs	Wayss/Wieghs	Ways/Weighs
188.	Molle/Mewl	Mulle/Mewl	Mole/Mewl	Mule/Mewl
189.	For/Four/Fore	For/Foor/Fore	Forr/Foor/Fore	Forr/Four/Fore
190.	Knead/Kneed	Knaed/Kned	Knead/Kned	Knaed/Kneed
191.	Gate/Giat	Gate/Gait	Gatte/Gait	Gatte/Giat
192.	Nay/Niegh	Nay/Neagh	Nay/Naegh	Nay/Neigh
193.	Attom/Adam	Attum/Adam	Atom/Adam	Atum/Adam
194.	Ourr/Hoor	Our/Hoor	Our/Hour	Ourr/Hour
195.	Whirrled/Wurld	Whirled/World	Whirrled/World	Whirled/Wurld
196.	Bibble/Babel	Babble/Babel	Bible/Babel	Bable/Babel

197.	Canvas/Canvass	Canvas/Canvas	Canvas/Canvasc	Cinvas/Canvas
198.	Fold/Foaled	Fulld/Foaled	Fuld/Foaled	Folld/Foaled
199.	Wave/Wiave	Wave/Waive	Wave/Waave	Wive/Waave
200.	Arc/Ark	Arc/Arck	Arrc/Ark	Arrc/Arck

Commonly misspelled words that sound alike but are spelled differently

Carefully circle the correct spelling combinations of words.

	A	B	C	D
1.	Navall/Navel	Nivall/Navel	Naval/Navel	Nival/Navel
2.	Moose/Moose	Moosse/Moose	Mousse/Moose	Mouse/Moose
3.	Been/Bin	Bean/Bin	Ben/Bin	Ben/Ban
4.	Orroile/Aureole	Oriole/Aureole	Oroile/Aureole	Orriole/Aureole
5.	Cllaque/Clack	Cllaque/Clak	Claque/Clack	Claque/Clak
6.	Churral/Coral	Chorral/Coral	Choral/Coral	Chural/Coral
7.	Greys/Graze	Grays/Graze	Grreys/Graze	Grrays/Graze
8.	Cedar/Seeder	Cedar/Seder	Cedar/Seader	Cedir/Seder
9.	Rung/Wrrung	Rung/Wrung	Rong/Wrrung	Rong/Wrung
10.	Baech/Bech	Beach/Bech	Baech/Beech	Beach/Beech
11.	Whurrled/World/Whirled	Whurled/World/Whirled	Whorrled/World/Whirled	Whorled/World/Whirled
12.	Meateir/Meteor	Meatier/Meteor	Meattier/Meteor	Meatteir/Meteor
13.	Fir/For	Firr/For	Fir/Fur	Firr/Fur
14.	Huarrd/Horde	Hoarrd/Horde	Huard/Horde	Hoard/Horde
15.	Sundae/Sunday	Sondea/Sunday	Sondae/Sunday	Sundea/Sunday
16.	Tiry/Terry	Tary/Terry	Tirry/Terry	Tarry/Terry
17.	Basis/Baces	Basis/Bases	Bascis/Bases	Bassis/Bases
18.	Graft/Graphed	Grapht/Graphed	Grrapht/Graphed	Grraft/Graphed
19.	Tendss/Tens	Tends/Tens	Tendsc/Tens	Tands/Tens
20.	Buy/By/Bye	Boy/By/Be	Buy/By/Be	Boy/By/Bye
21.	Wrapped/Rapped	Wripped/Rapped	Wriped/Rapped	Wraped/Rapped
22.	Weyne/Wain/Wane	Wayne/Wain/Wane	Wayne/Waan/Wane	Weyne/Waan/Wane

23.	To/Too/Two	Tu/To/Two	To/To/Two	To/Tou/Two
24.	Fette/Fate	Fette/Fite	Fete/Fite	Fete/Fate
25.	Rael/Reel	Real/Rel	Real/Reel	Rael/Rel
26.	Daul/Duel	Duall/Duel	Dual/Duel	Daull/Duel
27.	Mete/Maet/Meet	Mete/Maet/Met	Mete/Meat/Met	Mete/Meat/Meet
28.	Pian/Pane	Pain/Pane	Pain/Pan	Paan/Pane
29.	Musel/Muscle	Mussel/Mussle	Mussel/Muscle	Musel/Mussle
30.	Hial/Hale	Hail/Hale	Haill/Hale	Hiall/Hale
31.	Nit/Knit	Natt/Knit	Nat/Knit	Nitt/Knit
32.	Som/Some	Som/Soe	Sum/Soe	Sum/Some
33.	Minttel/Mantle	Mantel/Mantle	Mintel/Mantle	Manttel/Mantle
34.	Mean/Maen	Mean/Mein	Mean/Mien	Mean/Mean
35.	Tha/The	The/Thee	The/The	The/Thea
36.	Gene/Jein	Gene/Jean	Gene/Jien	Gene/Jaen
37.	Wrring/Ring	Wring/Ring	Wrang/Ring	Wrrang/Ring
38.	Bury/Berry	Bury/Bery	Bory/Berry	Bory/Bery
39.	Rigjer/Rigor	Riger/Rigor	Rigger/Rigor	Rijer/Rigor
40.	Barren/Baron	Barren/Barun	Baren/Baron	Baren/Barun
41.	Sachett/Sashay	Sachett/Sashey	Sachet/Sashay	Sachet/Sashey
42.	Carrot/Caret	Carrut/Caret	Carot/Caret	Carut/Caret
43.	Cue/Quea	Cue/Queue	Coe/Queue	Cue/Quee
44.	Gel/Jel	Gel/Jell	Gal/Jell	Gal/Jel
45.	Lian/Lane	Lain/Lane	Lain/Lan	Laan/Lane
46.	Riped/Rapt/Wrapped	Rapped/Rapt/Wrapped	Ripped/Rapt/Wrapped	Raped/Rapt/Wrapped
47.	Curcer/Cursor	Currser/Cursor	Curser/Cursor	Currcer/Cursor
48.	Manner/Manor	Maner/Manur	Maner/Manor	Manner/Manur
49.	Suede/Sweyed	Soede/Swayed	Suede/Swayed	Soede/Sweyed
50.	Jam/Gm	Jim/Gym	Jam/Gym	Jim/Gm
51.	Cascter/Castor	Caster/Castor	Caster/Castur	Casster/Castor

52.	Crrepe/Cripe	Crrepe/Crape	Crepe/Cripe	Crepe/Crape
53.	Owe/h	Owe/Oh	Owa/Oh	Owa/h
54.	Hoarse/Horse	Hoarrce/Horse	Hoarrse/Horse	Hoarce/Horse
55.	Bussed/Bust	Bused/Bust	Buced/Bust	Busced/Bust
56.	Grease/Greece	Graese/Grece	Grease/Grece	Graese/Greece
57.	Brayed/Braid	Breyed/Braid	Brreyed/Braid	Brrayed/Braid
58.	Exsed/Accede	Excead/Accede	Exced/Accede	Exceed/Accede
59.	Wrrak/Rack	Wrak/Rack	Wrack/Rack	Wrrack/Rack
60.	Grraham/Gram	Griham/Gram	Graham/Gram	Grriham/Gram
61.	Sync/Sink	Sync/Sinck	Sync/Sik	Sync/Sick
62.	Craek/Crek	Creak/Creek	Creak/Crek	Craek/Creek
63.	Cowarrd/Cowered	Coward/Cowered	Cuward/Cowered	Cuwarrd/Cowered
64.	Wane/Whine	Wine/Whine	Wine/Whie	Wine/Whei
65.	Whop/Houp	Whoup/Hoop	Whoop/Hoop	Whop/Hoop
66.	Bail/Bale/Baal	Bail/Bale/Bal	Bial/Bale/Baal	Bial/Bale/Bal
67.	Roogh/Ruff	Rough/Ruff	Rough/Ruf	Roogh/Ruf
68.	Axes/Axis	Axess/Axis	Axes/Axas	Axesc/Axis
69.	Tearr/Tier	Tear/Teir	Tear/Tier	Tearr/Teir
70.	I'd/Eyad	I'd/Eyed	I'd/Eyd	I'd/Eyt
71.	Gaph/Gaffe	Gaphf/Gaffe	Gaff/Gaffe	Gaf/Gaffe
72.	Roox/Re	Roox/Rue	Roux/Rue	Roux/Re
73.	Wead/We'D	Wad/We'D	Weed/We'D	Wed/We'D
74.	Gaitt/Gate	Giat/Gate	Gait/Gate	Giatt/Gate
75.	Kio/Coy	Koi/Coy	Koi/Co	Kui/Coy
76.	Innumerable/Enumerable	Inumerible/Enumerable	Inumerable/Enumerable	Innumerible/Enumerable
77.	Which/Wittch	Whach/Wittch	Which/Witch	Whach/Witch
78.	Weather/Whether	Weatther/Whether	Waetther/Whether	Waether/Whether
79.	Whined/Wind/Wined	Whaned/Wind/Wined	Whaned/Wind/Wind	Whined/Wind/Wind
80.	Hour/Our	Hourr/Our	Hoorr/Our	Hoor/Our

81.	Abell/Able	Abal/Able	Abel/Able	Aball/Able
82.	Axel/Axle	Axall/Axle	Axal/Axle	Axell/Axle
83.	Nose/Knows	Nouse/Knows	Nousse/Knows	Nosse/Knows
84.	Ruf/Rough	Ruff/Rough	Ruff/Roogh	Ruf/Roogh
85.	Fisher/Fisore	Fisher/Fiscure	Fisher/Fisure	Fisher/Fissure
86.	Curant/Current	Currant/Current	Corrant/Current	Corant/Current
87.	Steak/Stake	Staek/Stake	Sttaek/Stake	Stteak/Stake
88.	Chic/Shieck	Chic/Sheick	Chic/Sheik	Chic/Shiek
89.	Doe/Dew/Do	Due/Dew/Do	Due/Dew/o	Doe/Dew/o
90.	Wrapper/Rapper	Wripper/Rapper	Wriper/Rapper	Wraper/Rapper
91.	Grrayed/Grade	Grayed/Grade	Greyed/Grade	Grreyed/Grade
92.	Adduse/Educe	Adduce/Educe	Aduce/Educe	Aduse/Educe
93.	Frair/Fryer	Friar/Fryer	Frrair/Fryer	Frriar/Fryer
94.	Wax/Whaks	Wax/Whacksc	Wax/Whackss	Wax/Whacks
95.	Owad/Ode	Owad/Oe	Owed/Oe	Owed/Ode
96.	Rowed/Road/Rode	Ruwed/Road/Roe	Ruwed/Road/Rode	Rowed/Road/Roe
97.	Brood/Brewed	Broud/Brewed	Brud/Brewed	Brod/Brewed
98.	Fatte/Fete	Fate/Fete	Fitte/Fete	Fite/Fete
99.	Gnies/Nice	Gneis/Nice	Gneiss/Nice	Gniess/Nice
100.	Mind/Mind	Mind/Mined	Mand/Mined	Mand/Mind
101.	You/Yew/Ewe	Yoo/Yew/Ewe	You/Yew/Ee	Yoo/Yew/Ee
102.	Goilt/Gilt	Guilt/Gilt	Guillt/Gilt	Goillt/Gilt
103.	Ascent/Asent	Assent/Asent	Ascent/Assent	Assent/Assent
104.	Wue/Whoa	Wue/Wha	Woe/Whoa	Woe/Wha
105.	Grade/Greyed	Grade/Grayed	Grrade/Grayed	Grrade/Greyed
106.	Furrward/Foreword	Forrward/Foreword	Forward/Foreword	Furward/Foreword
107.	Tue/Tow	Toe/Tow	Tue/Tw	Toe/Tw
108.	Wade/Weaghed	Wade/Waeghed	Wade/Weighed	Wade/Wieghed
109.	Impasable/Impassible	Impassable/Impassable	Impassable/Impassible	Impasable/Impassable

110.	Bee/Be	Bea/Be	Be/Be	Ba/Be
111.	Thaa/Tei	Thaa/Tie	Thai/Tei	Thai/Tie
112.	Straightened/Straitened	Striaghtened/Straitened	Sttraightened/Straitened	Sttriaghtened/Straitened
113.	Maze/Maaze	Mize/Maaze	Maze/Miaze	Maze/Maize
114.	Heroin/Heroine	Herroin/Heroine	Herrion/Heroine	Herion/Heroine
115.	Reveiw/Revue	Review/Revoe	Review/Revue	Reveiw/Revoe
116.	Musce/Mews	Musse/Mews	Muse/Mews	Muce/Mews
117.	Staid/Stayed	Sttaid/Steyed	Staid/Steyed	Sttaid/Stayed
118.	Grrater/Graeter	Grater/Graeter	Grrater/Greater	Grater/Greater
119.	We/Wea	We/Wee	Wa/We	We/We
120.	Bascal/Basil	Basal/Basal	Bassal/Basil	Basal/Basil
121.	Addition/Edition	Adition/Edition	Additoin/Edition	Aditoin/Edition
122.	Symbull/Cymbal	Symbul/Cymbal	Symbol/Cymbal	Symboll/Cymbal
123.	One/Wun	One/Wn	Ona/Wn	One/Won
124.	Wunt/Want	Wont/Want	Wontt/Want	Wuntt/Want
125.	Capittal/Capitul	Capittal/Capitol	Capital/Capitol	Capital/Capitul
126.	Harre/Higher	Hire/Higher	Hirre/Higher	Hare/Higher
127.	Bridal/Bridle	Bradal/Bridle	Brradal/Bridle	Brridal/Bridle
128.	Bard/Barred	Bard/Bared	Bird/Bared	Bird/Barred
129.	Basces/Basis	Basses/Basis	Bases/Basis	Baces/Basis
130.	Rabbet/Rabbat	Rabet/Rabbat	Rabbet/Rabbit	Rabet/Rabbit
131.	Faet/Feet	Faet/Fet	Feat/Fet	Feat/Feet
132.	We'd/Weed	Wa'd/Wed	We'd/Wead	We'd/Wed
133.	Mod/Moued	Moud/Mooed	Mood/Mooed	Mod/Mooed
134.	Wial/Whale/Wale	Wail/Whale/Wale	Waill/Whale/Wale	Wiall/Whale/Wale
135.	Yoo'l/Yule	Yoo'll/Yule	You'll/Yule	You'l/Yule
136.	Wittch/Which	Witch/Which	Watch/Which	Wattch/Which
137.	Lacksc/Lax	Lacks/Lax	Laks/Lax	Lackss/Lax
138.	Mrs./Misces	Mrs./Misses	Mrs./Mises	Mrs./Mices

139.	Waderr/Waiter	Wader/Waiter	Wader/Wiater	Waderr/Wiater
140.	Greece/Grease	Greece/Graese	Grece/Grease	Grece/Graese
141.	Beer/Bier	Ber/Bier	Beer/Beir	Ber/Beir
142.	Waive/Wave	Wiave/Wave	Waive/Wav	Waave/Wave
143.	Baerr/Bare	Bear/Bare	Baer/Bare	Bearr/Bare
144.	Allowed/Aloud	Alowed/Alood	Allowed/Alood	Alowed/Aloud
145.	Adam/Atom	Adam/Attum	Adam/Attom	Adam/Atum
146.	Through/Threw	Thrroogh/Threw	Thrrough/Threw	Throogh/Threw
147.	Goild/Gild	Guild/Gild	Goilld/Gild	Guilld/Gild
148.	Crawl/Kral	Criwl/Kral	Criwl/Kraal	Crawl/Kraal
149.	Faw/Phew	Few/Phew	Faw/Phw	Few/Phw
150.	Swayed/Suede	Sweyed/Suede	Swayed/Soede	Sweyed/Soede
151.	Threw/Through	Thrrew/Throogh	Thrrew/Through	Threw/Throogh
152.	Role/Roll	Role/Rol	Rule/Rol	Rule/Roll
153.	Foregone/Forgone	Furregone/Forgone	Furegone/Forgone	Forregone/Forgone
154.	Wearrs/Wares/Where's	Waers/Wares/Where's	Waerrs/Wares/Where's	Wears/Wares/Where's
155.	Ads/Adds	Ads/Ads	Ads/Adde	Adt/Ads
156.	Rouse/Rows	Rose/Rows	Rosse/Rows	Rousse/Rows
157.	Frieze/Frees/Freeze	Frieze/Fres/Freeze	Freize/Fres/Freeze	Freize/Frees/Freeze
158.	Naegh/Nay	Neigh/Nay	Neagh/Nay	Niegh/Nay
159.	Burjer/Burgher	Burger/Burgher	Burrger/Burgher	Burrjer/Burgher
160.	Facts/Fax	Fictts/Fax	Factts/Fax	Ficts/Fax
161.	Wale/Wail/Whale	Wale/Wial/Whale	Walle/Wail/Whale	Walle/Wial/Whale
162.	Might/Mite	Maght/Mite	Maghtt/Mite	Mightt/Mite
163.	Gillder/Goilder	Gilder/Guilder	Gilder/Goilder	Gillder/Guilder
164.	Bawled/Bald/Baled	Bawled/Bald/Balled	Biwled/Bald/Balled	Biwled/Bald/Baled
165.	Heel/He'll/Heal	Heel/He'll/Hael	Hel/He'll/Hael	Hel/He'll/Heal
166.	Grraphed/Graft	Graphed/Grapht	Grraphed/Grapht	Graphed/Graft
167.	Choose/Chew	Chouse/Chews	Choose/Chews	Chose/Chews

168.	Nightt/Knight	Naghtt/Knight	Naght/Knight	Night/Knight
169.	Where/Ware/Wear	Wherre/Ware/Wear	Wherre/Ware/Waer	Where/Ware/Waer
170.	Courrser/Coarser	Courser/Coarser	Coorser/Coarser	Coorrser/Coarser
171.	Hangarr/Hanger	Hangar/Hanger	Hangar/Hanjer	Hangarr/Hanjer
172.	Wantt/Wont	Wantt/Wunt	Want/Wont	Want/Wunt
173.	Lay/Lae	Lay/Lei	Lay/Lea	Lay/Lie
174.	Inssight/Incite	Insaght/Incite	Insight/Incite	Inscight/Incite
175.	Steyed/Staid	Stayed/Staid	Stteyed/Staid	Sttayed/Staid
176.	Room/Rheum	Rom/Rheom	Roum/Rheum	Rom/Rheum
177.	Whule/Hole	Whole/Hole	Wholle/Hole	Whulle/Hole
178.	Bot/But	But/But	Bot/Butt	But/Butt
179.	Warrn/Worn	Warn/Wurn	Warn/Worn	Warrn/Wurn
180.	Fendss/Fens	Fends/Fens	Fands/Fens	Fendsc/Fens
181.	Hal/Hual	Hall/Hual	Hall/Haul	Hal/Haul
182.	Hurts/Hertz	Horts/Hertz	Hurrts/Hertz	Horrts/Hertz
183.	Tide/Tied	Tade/Tied	Tade/Teid	Tide/Teid
184.	Krrapht/Craft	Krraft/Craft	Kraft/Craft	Krapht/Craft
185.	Gibe/Jie	Gibe/Jibe	Gabe/Jibe	Gibe/Jei
186.	Maet/Met/Mete	Meat/Meet/Mete	Maet/Meet/Mete	Meat/Met/Mete
187.	Lek/Leak	Leek/Laek	Leek/Leak	Lek/Laek
188.	Mal/Mil	Mil/Mill	Mal/Mill	Mil/Mil
189.	Gnome/Noe	Gnume/Noe	Gnome/Nome	Gnume/Nome
190.	Rack/Wrack	Rak/Wrrack	Rak/Wrack	Rack/Wrrack
191.	Lays/Laze/Leis	Layss/Laze/Leis	Layss/Laze/Lies	Lays/Laze/Lies
192.	Mark/Marc	Marrk/Marc	Marck/Marc	Marrck/Marc
193.	Wane/Wayne/Wain	Wane/Weyne/Wain	Wane/Wayne/Waan	Wane/Weyne/Waan
194.	Thrrown/Throne	Thrown/Throne	Thrruwn/Throne	Thruwn/Throne
195.	Tae/Te	Tea/Te	Tea/Tee	Tae/Tee
196.	Read/Reed	Read/Red	Raed/Red	Raed/Reed

Commonly misspelled words that sound alike but are spelled differently

Carefully circle the correct spelling combinations of words.

	A	B	C	D
1.	Metle/Meddle/Medil	Metle/Meddle/Medal	Mettle/Meddle/Medil	Mettle/Meddle/Medal
2.	Knive/Nave	Knave/Nae	Knave/Nea	Knave/Nave
3.	Roam/Rome	Roam/Roe	Ruam/Roe	Ruam/Rome
4.	Wheel/We'll	Whal/We'll	Whel/We'll	Wheal/We'll
5.	Red/Read	Reed/Read	Reed/Raed	Red/Raed
6.	Holle/Whole	Hole/Whole	Hule/Whole	Hulle/Whole
7.	Must/Mused	Must/Musced	Must/Muced	Must/Mussed
8.	Hive/Halve	Have/Halve	Hive/Hallve	Have/Hallve
9.	Aal/Ale	Ail/Ale	Aall/Ale	Aill/Ale
10.	Lands/Lens	Lends/Lens	Lendss/Lens	Lendsc/Lens
11.	Rumor/Roomer	Romor/Romer	Rumor/Roumer	Rumor/Romer
12.	Tuaghtt/Taut	Taughtt/Taut	Taught/Taut	Tuaght/Taut
13.	Whar/Were	Whir/Were	Whirr/Were	Wharr/Were
14.	Causse/Caws	Cause/Caws	Cuasse/Caws	Cuase/Caws
15.	Bia/Bah	Ba/Bah	Baa/Bah	Bi/Bah
16.	Wore/War	Worre/War	Wurre/War	Wure/War
17.	Nivell/Naval	Navel/Naval	Navell/Naval	Nivel/Naval
18.	Wieghtt/Wait	Weight/Wait	Wieght/Wait	Weightt/Wait
19.	Eve/Eave	Eve/Eea	Eve/Eive	Eve/Eae
20.	Mucoos/Mucus	Mucooss/Mucus	Mucouss/Mucus	Mucous/Mucus
21.	Rapper/Wrapper	Ripper/Wrapper	Raper/Wrapper	Riper/Wrapper
22.	Graeter/Grater	Grreater/Grater	Greater/Grater	Grraeter/Grater

23.	Duked/Duct	Duked/Ductt	Ducked/Duct	Ducked/Ductt
24.	Roe/Rw	Rue/Rw	Rue/Row	Roe/Row
25.	Carul/Carrel	Carol/Carel	Carol/Carrel	Carul/Carel
26.	Tooter/Tudor/Tutor	Toter/Todor/Tutor	Touter/Tudor/Tutor	Toter/Tudor/Tutor
27.	Theirr/There/They're	Thierr/There/They're	Their/There/They're	Thier/There/They're
28.	Itt's/Its	It's/Itst	Ittts/Its	It's/Its
29.	Marrshal/Martail	Marshal/Martail	Marshal/Martial	Marrshal/Martial
30.	Suit/Soot	Soit/Sot	Suit/Sout	Suit/Sot
31.	Chek/Czech	Check/Czeh	Chek/Czeh	Check/Czech
32.	Casct/Caste	Casst/Caste	Cast/Caste	Cist/Caste
33.	Adherence/Adherents	Adherrence/Adherents	Adherrance/Adherents	Adherance/Adherents
34.	Sashay/Sachet	Sasshay/Sachet	Sashey/Sachet	Sasshey/Sachet
35.	Cilendar/Calender	Cillendar/Calender	Callendar/Calender	Calendar/Calender
36.	Actts/Ax	Aclts/Ax	Acts/sx	Acts/Ax
37.	Gourrd/Gored	Goord/Gored	Gourd/Gored	Goorrd/Gored
38.	Arant/Errant	Arrint/Errant	Arint/Errant	Arrant/Errant
39.	Eyed/Id	Eyed/I'd	Eyad/Id	Eyad/I'd
40.	Heys/Haze	Hayss/Haze	Heyss/Haze	Hays/Haze
41.	Burro/Burrow/Boroogh	Buro/Burrow/Borough	Burro/Burrow/Borough	Buro/Burrow/Boroogh
42.	Tued/Towed/Tod	Toed/Towed/Toad	Toed/Towed/Tod	Tued/Towed/Toad
43.	Alle/Ail	Ale/Aal	Ale/Ail	Alle/Aal
44.	Goilder/Gilder	Goillder/Gilder	Guillder/Gilder	Guilder/Gilder
45.	Foull/Fowl	Fool/Fowl	Fooll/Fowl	Foul/Fowl
46.	Paill/Pale	Piall/Pale	Pail/Pale	Pial/Pale
47.	Rain/Riegn/Rein	Rain/Reign/Rein	Raan/Riegn/Rein	Raan/Reign/Rein
48.	Wrry/Rya	Wry/Rye	Wry/Rya	Wrry/Rye
49.	Aasle/Isle	Aiscle/Isle	Aisle/Isle	Aissle/Isle
50.	Told/Tolled	Told/Toled	Tuld/Tolled	Tuld/Toled
51.	No/Know	Nu/Knw	Nu/Know	No/Knw

52.	Warre/Waer/Where	Ware/Waer/Where	Warre/Wear/Where	Ware/Wear/Where
53.	Wrong/Rung	Wrrong/Rung	Wrung/Rung	Wrrung/Rung
54.	Miscal/Missile	Misal/Miscile	Misal/Missile	Missal/Missile
55.	Bad/Bade	Bad/Bea	Bad/Bae	Bid/Bade
56.	They're/Their/There	They'rre/Thier/There	They're/Thier/There	They'rre/Their/There
57.	Bind/Banned	Band/Baned	Band/Banned	Bind/Baned
58.	Won/Oe	Wun/Oe	Won/One	Wun/One
59.	Head/He'd	Had/He'd	Heed/He'd	Hed/He'd
60.	Sttyle/Stile	Sttyle/Stale	Style/Stile	Style/Stale
61.	Brech/Braech	Brech/Breach	Breech/Breach	Breech/Braech
62.	Matter/Madder	Mitter/Madder	Miter/Madder	Mater/Madder
63.	Biated/Bated	Baitted/Bated	Biatted/Bated	Baited/Bated
64.	Cygnett/Signet	Cygnett/Sagnet	Cygnet/Sagnet	Cygnet/Signet
65.	Who's/Whose	Who'ss/Whose	Who'ss/Whouse	Who's/Whouse
66.	Booy/By	Booy/Boy	Buoy/By	Buoy/Boy
67.	Stiar/Stare	Sttiar/Stare	Sttair/Stare	Stair/Stare
68.	Wrrate/Right/Rite	Wrate/Right/Rite	Wrrite/Right/Rite	Write/Right/Rite
69.	Laech/Lech	Leach/Lech	Leach/Leech	Laech/Leech
70.	Bazaar/Bazarre	Bazaar/Bizarre	Bazar/Bizarre	Bazar/Bazarre
71.	Cielling/Sealing	Ceilling/Sealing	Ceiling/Sealing	Cieling/Sealing
72.	Al/Awl	All/Asl	AlqAwl	All/Awl
73.	Furt/Forte	Fort/Forte	Furrt/Forte	Forrt/Forte
74.	Censor/Sensor	Censsor/Sensor	Censcor/Sensor	Censur/Sensor
75.	Cheap/Chep	Cheap/Cheep	Chaep/Cheep	Chaep/Chep
76.	Maddle	Madle	Meqle	Meddle
77.	Lied/Led	Lead/Led	Laed/Led	Leid/Led
78.	Haerr/Here	Hear/Here	Hearr/Here	Haer/Here
79.	Apatate/Apetite	Apatite/Apetite	Apatate/Appetite	Apatite/Appetite
80.	Whale/Wale/Wail	Whalle/Wale/Wail	Whale/Wale/Wial	Whalle/Wale/Wial

81.	Tense/Tents	Tensse/Tents	Tence/Tents	Tensce/Tents
82.	Reagn/Rien/Rain	Reagn/Rein/Rain	Riegn/Rein/Rain	Reign/Rein/Rain
83.	Beir/Beer	Beir/Ber	Bier/Ber	Bier/Beer
84.	Grall/Grille	Grill/Grille	Gral/Grille	Gril/Grille
85.	Kernel/Culonel	Kernel/Colonel	Kerrnel/Colonel	Kerrnel/Culonel
86.	Where'S/Waers/Wares	Where'S/Wears/Wares	Wherre'S/Waers/Wares	Wherre'S/Wears/Wares
87.	Rume/Rom	Rume/Roam	Rome/Roam	Rome/Rom
88.	Roe/Roux	Roe/Roox	Rue/Roux	Rue/Roox
89.	Fix/Factts	Fax/Factts	Fax/Facts	Fix/Facts
90.	Cellir/Seller	Celir/Seller	Celar/Seller	Cellar/Seller
91.	Hiy/Hay	Hiy/Hey	Hay/Hay	Hay/Hey
92.	Cllew/Cloe	Clew/Cloe	Cllew/Clue	Clew/Clue
93.	Orre/Oar/Or	Ore/Oar/Or	Orre/Oir/Or	Ore/Oir/Or
94.	New/Gno/Knew	New/Gnu/Knw	New/Gno/Knw	New/Gnu/Knew
95.	Cluase/Claws	Clluase/Claws	Cllause/Claws	Clause/Claws
96.	Raghtt/Rite/Write	Right/Rite/Write	Raght/Rite/Write	Rightt/Rite/Write
97.	Whirred/Word	Whirred/Wurd	Whired/Word	Whired/Wurd
98.	Rap/Wrrap	Rip/Wrrap	Rap/Wrap	Rip/Wrap
99.	Hagher/Hire	Hagherr/Hire	Higherr/Hire	Higher/Hire
100.	Barre/Bear	Bare/Baer	Bare/Bear	Barre/Baer
101.	Rast/Wrest	Resst/Wrest	Rest/Wrest	Resct/Wrest
102.	Fur/Fir	Furr/Fir	For/Fir	Forr/Fir
103.	Brrows/Browce	Brrows/Browse	Brows/Browce	Brows/Browse
104.	Row/Roe	Ruw/Re	Row/Re	Ruw/Roe
105.	Nutt/Knot	Nut/Knot	Nott/Knot	Not/Knot
106.	Chille/Chili	Chale/Chili	Challe/Chili	Chile/Chili
107.	Paced/Paste	Paced/Passte	Paced/Pascte	Pased/Paste
108.	Hairr/Hare	Hair/Hare	Hiar/Hare	Hiarr/Hare
109.	Hostel/Hostile	Houstel/Hostile	Hosstel/Hostile	Housstel/Hostile

110.	Balm/Bumb	Ballm/Bomb	Balm/Bomb	Ballm/Bumb
111.	Pidded/Patted	Pided/Patted	Paded/Patted	Padded/Patted
112.	Wand/Wined/Whind	Wind/Wined/Whined	Wind/Wined/Whind	Wand/Wined/Whined
113.	Sari/Sury	Sari/Sory	Sari/Surry	Sari/Sorry
114.	Weighss/Ways	Wieghss/Ways	Wieghs/Ways	Weighs/Ways
115.	Ruad/Rode/Rowed	Road/Rode/Rowd	Ruad/Rode/Rowd	Road/Rode/Rowed
116.	Ayes/Eyes	Ayas/Eyes	Ayesc/Eyes	Ayess/Eyes
117.	Stap/Steppe	Stap/Stepe	Step/Stepe	Step/Steppe
118.	Leech/Laech	Lech/Leach	Lech/Laech	Leech/Leach
119.	Gno/Knew/New	Gnu/Knew/New	Gnu/Knew/Nw	Gno/Knew/Nw
120.	Leak/Lek	Laek/Leek	Leak/Leek	Laek/Lek
121.	Airr/Hier	Air/Heir	Airr/Heir	Air/Hier
122.	Halle/Hail	Halle/Hial	Hale/Hail	Hale/Hial
123.	Sttake/Staek	Stake/Staek	Stake/Steak	Sttake/Steak
124.	Knows/Nose	Knowss/Nouse	Knows/Nouse	Knowss/Nose
125.	I'll/Aasle/Isle	I'l/Aasle/Isle	I'll/Aisle/Isle	I'l/Aisle/Isle
126.	Moat/Mote	Muat/Mote	Muatt/Mote	Moatt/Mote
127.	Fil/Phil	Fall/Phil	Fill/Phil	Fal/Phil
128.	Mises/Mrs.	Misses/Mrs.	Mices/Mrs.	Misces/Mrs.
129.	Franc/Frank	Frranc/Frank	Frranc/Franck	Franc/Franck
130.	Were/Whar	Werre/Whir	Werre/Whar	Were/Whir
131.	Gail/Gale	Gaill/Gale	Giall/Gale	Gial/Gale
132.	Nun/None	Non/None	Nun/Noe	Non/Noe
133.	Gamble/Gambul	Gamblle/Gambul	Gamble/Gambol	Gamblle/Gambol
134.	Atte/Eight	Ate/Eaght	Atte/Eaght	Ate/Eight
135.	Beter/Bettor	Beter/Bettur	Better/Bettur	Better/Bettor
136.	Lessen/Lesson	Lesen/Lescon	Lesen/Lesson	Lescen/Lesson
137.	Would/Wood	Would/Wod	Woold/Wod	Woold/Wood
138.	Aye/Eyel	Aye/Eye/I	Aya/Eyel	Aya/Eye/I

139.	Hu/He	Ho/He	Hu/Hoe	Ho/Hoe
140.	Fanish/Finish	Finish/Finnish	Fanish/Finnish	Finish/Finish
141.	Brews/Bruice	Brews/Bruise	Brrews/Bruice	Brrews/Bruise
142.	Insstence/Instants	Instance/Instants	Insstance/Instants	Instence/Instants
143.	Mude/Mowed	Mode/Mowed	Mode/Mowd	Mude/Mowd
144.	Canter/Cantur	Cantter/Cantor	Canter/Cantor	Cantter/Cantur
145.	Horrse/Hoarse	Horrce/Hoarse	Horce/Hoarse	Horse/Hoarse
146.	Thyme/Tei	Thyme/Time	Thyme/Tame	Thyme/Tie
147.	Mised/Mist	Misced/Mist	Missed/Mist	Miced/Mist
148.	Incite/Insight	Incate/Insight	Incitte/Insight	Incatte/Insight
149.	Be/Be	Be/Bee	Ba/Be	Be/Bea
150.	Musctard/Mustered N	Musstard/Mustered	Mostard/Mustered	Mustard/Mustered
151.	Bawl/Ball	Biwl/Bal	Biwl/Ball	Bawl/Bal
152.	Oda/Owd	Ode/Owed	Oda/Owed	Ode/Owd
153.	Bassk/Basque	Bask/Basqu	Basck/Basque	Bask/Basque
154.	Illusive/Allusive/Elusive	Ilosive/Allusive/Elusive	Ilusive/Allusive/Elusive	Illosive/Allusive/Elusive
155.	Misile/Miscal	Miscile/Missal	Misile/Missal	Missile/Missal
156.	Bet/Baet	Beet/Baet	Beet/Beat	Bet/Beat
157.	Fairr/Fare	Fair/Fare	Fiar/Fare	Fiarr/Fare
158.	Mat/Mate	Mit/Matte	Mat/Matte	Mit/Mate
159.	Crews/Cruise	Crrews/Cruise	Crrews/Cruice	Crews/Cruice
160.	Liess/Lays/Laze	Leiss/Lays/Laze	Leis/Lays/Laze	Lies/Lays/Laze
161.	Mayorr/Mare	Mayor/Mare	Meyor/Mare	Meyorr/Mare
162.	Yocke/Yolk	Yocke/Yollk	Yoke/Yolk	Yoke/Yollk
163.	Ned/Knead/Kneed	Need/Knead/Kneed	Need/Knaed/Kneed	Ned/Knaed/Kneed
164.	Sack/Sc	Sak/Sc	Sak/Sac	Sack/Sac
165.	Wreak/Rek	Wraek/Reek	Wreak/Reek	Wraek/Rek
166.	Cede/Sed	Cade/Sed	Cede/Seed	Cede/Sead
167.	Aurral/Oral	Aural/Oral	Aorral/Oral	Aoral/Oral

168.	Aureole/Oriole	Aurreole/Oroile	Aureole/Oroile	Aurreole/Oriole
169.	Away/Aweagh	Away/Aweigh	Away/Awaegh	Away/Awiegh
170.	Awl/Al	Awl/Al	Awl/All	Awc/All
171.	Galle/Gial	Galle/Gail	Gale/Gail	Gale/Gial
172.	Lee/Lae	Lee/Lea	Le/Lae	Le/Lea
173.	Ductt/Duked	Duct/Duked	Duct/Ducked	Ductt/Ducked
174.	Waitt/Wieght	Wait/Wieght	Wait/Weight	Waitt/Weight
175.	Palate/Palette/Pallet	Palate/Palete/Pallet	Pilate/Palete/Pallet	Pilate/Palette/Pallet
176.	Hay/Hay	Hay/Hiy	Hey/Hiy	Hey/Hay
177.	Base/Basc	Base/Bas	Bace/Bas	Base/Bass
178.	Sttile/Style	Stile/Style	Sttale/Style	Stale/Style
179.	Casch/Cache	Cash/Cache	Cish/Cache	Cassh/Cache
180.	Jean/Gene	Jein/Gene	Jien/Gene	Jaen/Gene
181.	Tern/Turn	Terrn/Torn	Tern/Torn	Terrn/Turn
182.	Auger/Augur	Aujerr/Augur	Aujer/Augur	Augerr/Augur
183.	Warr/Wure	War/Wure	War/Wore	Warr/Wore
184.	Wares/Where's/Waers	Warres/Where's/Wears	Warres/Where's/Waers	Wares/Where's/Wears
185.	In/Iz	In/Ian	In/In	In/Inn
186.	Muwed/Moe	Mowed/Mode	Mowed/Moe	Muwed/Mode
187.	Ferry/Fairy	Ferry/Fiary	Fery/Fiary	Fery/Fairy
188.	Nice/Gneis	Nice/Gneiss	Nice/Gniess	Nice/Gnies
189.	Clack/Claque	Cllack/Claque	Clak/Claque	Cllak/Claque
190.	Whua/Woe	Whoa/Woe	Whua/We	Whoa/We
191.	Cruise/Crews	Crruice/Crews	Cruice/Crews	Crruise/Crews
192.	Mints/Mince	Mintts/Mince	Mintts/Minse	Mints/Minse
193.	Faintt/Feint	Faintt/Fient	Faint/Fient	Faint/Feint
194.	Wieve/We've	Waeve/We've	Weive/We've	Weave/We've
195.	Handmade/Handmaad	Handmade/Handmaid	Hindmade/Handmaad	Handmade/Handmiad

Commonly misspelled words that sound alike but are spelled differently

Carefully circle the correct spelling combinations of words.

	A	B	C	D
1.	Sun/Son	Son/Son	Son/Sn	Sun/Sn
2.	Hare/Hiar	Harre/Hiar	Harre/Hair	Hare/Hair
3.	Cache/Casch	Cache/Cash	Ciche/Cash	Cache/Cassh
4.	Cite/Sight	Citte/Sight	Cate/Sight	Catte/Sight
5.	Wurn/Warn	Worn/Warn	Worrn/Warn	Wurrn/Warn
6.	Minerr/Minor	Miner/Minor	Minerr/Minur	Miner/Minur
7.	Wrretch/Retch	Wretch/Retch	Wratch/Retch	Wrratch/Retch
8.	Flour/Flower	Floor/Flower	Fllour/Flower	Flloor/Flower
9.	Whalle/Wile	Whale/Wile	Whille/Wile	While/Wile
10.	Caloos/Callus	Calous/Callus	Calloos/Callus	Callous/Callus
11.	Boild/Billed	Boild/Biled	Build/Biled	Build/Billed
12.	Marrten/Martin	Marten/Martin	Marten/Martan	Marrten/Martan
13.	Humerus/Humoroos	Humerus/Humorous	Humerrus/Humoroos	Humerrus/Humorous
14.	Hose/Hoes	Housse/Hoes	Hosse/Hoes	House/Hoes
15.	Mey Be/Maybe	Miy Be/Meybe	May Be/Maybe	Miy Be/Maybe
16.	Metal/Metle/Meddle	Metal/Mettle/Meddle	Metil/Mettle/Meddle	Metil/Metle/Meddle
17.	Halve/Have	Hilve/Have	Hillve/Have	Hallve/Have
18.	Wa/We	We/We	Wee/We	Wea/We
19.	Taperr/Tapar	Taperr/Tapir	Taper/Tapar	Taper/Tapir
20.	Timber/Timbre	Tamberr/Timbre	Timberr/Timbre	Tamber/Timbre
21.	Mince/Mints	Minse/Mints	Minse/Mintts	Mince/Mintts
22.	Eyess/Ayes	Eyesc/Ayes	Eyes/Ayes	Eyas/Ayes

23.	Guesced/Guest	Guessed/Guest	Gueced/Guest	Guesed/Guest
24.	Yore/Yoor/You'Re	Yore/Your/You'Re	Yorre/Your/You'Re	Yorre/Yoor/You'Re
25.	Oarr/Or/Ore	Oir/Or/Ore	Oirr/Or/Ore	Oar/Or/Ore
26.	Batte/Bait	Bate/Biat	Batte/Biat	Bate/Bait
27.	Tax/Tackss	Tax/Taks	Tax/Tacksc	Tax/Tacks
28.	Bald/Balled/Bawled	Bild/Balled/Bawled	Bild/Baled/Bawled	Bald/Baled/Bawled
29.	Ewe/Yoo/Yew	Ewe/Yoo/Yw	Ewe/You/Yw	Ewe/You/Yew
30.	Eya/I/Ae	Eya/I/Aye	Eye/I/Ae	Eye/I/Aye
31.	Hoes/House	Hoess/House	Hoes/Hose	Hoess/Hose
32.	Tou/Two/To	To/Two/To	Too/Two/To	Tu/Two/To
33.	Cerres/Sereis	Ceres/Sereis	Ceres/Series	Cerres/Series
34.	Hansum/Handsome	Hanscom/Handsome	Hansom/Handsome	Hanssom/Handsome
35.	Ressidence/Residents	Ressidance/Residents	Residence/Residents	Residance/Residents
36.	Surph/Serf	Surf/Serf	Surrf/Serf	Surrph/Serf
37.	Sail/Sale	Saill/Sale	Siall/Sale	Sial/Sale
38.	There's/Thiers	Therre's/Theirs	There's/Theirs	Therre's/Thiers
39.	Rued/Rude	Rued/Rue	Roed/Rude	Roed/Rue
40.	Aid/Aei	Aid/Aide	Aid/Aie	Aad/Aide
41.	Team/Teem	Taem/Tem	Taem/Teem	Team/Tem
42.	Ilusion/Allusion	Illusoin/Allusion	Ilusoin/Allusion	Illusion/Allusion
43.	Hi/Hih	Ha/Hih	Ha/High	Hi/High
44.	Bired/Bard	Bared/Bard	Barred/Bard	Birred/Bard
45.	Mewl/Mole	Mewl/Mule	Mewll/Mule	Mewll/Mole
46.	Rowss/Rouse	Rows/Rouse	Rows/Rose	Rowss/Rose
47.	Cheep/Cheap	Chep/Chaep	Chep/Cheap	Cheep/Chaep
48.	Bih/Baa	Bih/Ba	Bah/Ba	Bah/Baa
49.	Goffer/Gopher	Gopher/Gopher	Gophfer/Gopher	Gofer/Gopher
50.	Dun/Doe	Dun/Done	Don/Doe	Don/Done
51.	Ratte/Write/Right	Rate/Write/Right	Ritte/Write/Right	Rite/Write/Right

52.	Mitte/Might	Mate/Might	Mite/Might	Matte/Might
53.	Litter/Ladder	Liter/Ladder	Later/Ladder	Latter/Ladder
54.	Gored/Goord	Gorred/Goord	Gored/Gourd	Gorred/Gourd
55.	Bell/Belle	Bel/Belle	Bal/Belle	Ball/Belle
56.	Rucell/Rustle	Rusell/Rustle	Russell/Rustle	Ruscell/Rustle
57.	Taut/Taught	Tuatt/Taught	Tuat/Taught	Tautt/Taught
58.	Cozen/Coosin	Cozen/Cousin	Cozen/Coussin	Cozen/Coossin
59.	Morn/Mourn	Morrn/Moorn	Morn/Moorn	Morrn/Mourn
60.	Sttare/Stair	Stare/Stiar	Stare/Stair	Sttare/Stiar
61.	Wrip/Rap	Wrrip/Rap	Wrrap/Rap	Wrap/Rap
62.	Cents/Scents	Centts/Scents	Centts/Ssents	Cents/Ssents
63.	Basste/Based	Baste/Based	Baste/Baced	Bascte/Based
64.	Four/Fore/For	Foorr/Fore/For	Fourr/Fore/For	Foor/Fore/For
65.	Knikerrs/Nickers	Knickers/Nickers	Knickerrs/Nickers	Knikers/Nickers
66.	Marre/Meyor	Mare/Meyor	Marre/Mayor	Mare/Mayor
67.	Surje/Serge	Surrge/Serge	Surrje/Serge	Surge/Serge
68.	Stael/Stel	Stael/Steel	Steal/Steel	Steal/Stel
69.	Haerrt/Hart	Hearrt/Hart	Heart/Hart	Haert/Hart
70.	Hulled/Hold	Holled/Hold	Holed/Hold	Huled/Hold
71.	Way/Weagh/Whey	Way/Waegh/Whey	Way/Wiegh/Whey	Way/Weigh/Whey
72.	Dyieng/Dying	Dyaeng/Dying	Dyeing/Dying	Dyeang/Dying
73.	Holay/Holy/Wholly	Holay/Holy/Wholy	Holey/Holy/Wholly	Holey/Holy/Wholly
74.	Sword/Soared	Sworrd/Soared	Swurrd/Soared	Swurd/Soared
75.	Cane/Cian	Cine/Caan	Cane/Cain	Cane/Caan
76.	Ariel/Aerial	Arreil/Aerial	Areil/Aerial	Arriel/Aerial
77.	Brot/Brute	Brrut/Brute	Brut/Brute	Brrot/Brute
78.	Frreys/Phrase	Frrays/Phrase	Frays/Phrase	Freys/Phrase
79.	Throne/Thrown	Thrune/Thrown	Thrrune/Thrown	Thrrone/Thrown
80.	He'd/Hed	Ha'd/Hed	He'd/Heed	He'd/Head

81.	Waer/Where/Ware	Wear/Where/Ware	Wearr/Where/Ware	Waerr/Where/Ware
82.	Braed/Bred	Brraed/Bred	Brread/Bred	Bread/Bred
83.	We've/Weave	We've/Waeve	We've/Wieve	We've/Weive
84.	Hew/Hoe/Huh	Hew/Hue/Huh	Hew/Hoe/Hugh	Hew/Hue/Hugh
85.	Nickers/Knickers	Nikerrs/Knickers	Nickerrs/Knickers	Nikers/Knickers
86.	Cell/Sell	Cel/Sell	Call/Sell	Cal/Sell
87.	Isle/I'l/Aisle	Isle/I'l/Aasle	Isle/I'll/Aasle	Isle/I'll/Aisle
88.	Brruise/Brews	Bruise/Brews	Brruice/Brews	Bruice/Brews
89.	Exsept/Accept	Except/Acept	Exsept/Acept	Except/Accept

Commonly Misspelled
Compound Words

Name: _____

Date: _____

Underarm	Keypunch	Moonshine	Dogwood	Earthbound	Newsstand
Sundown	Newborn	Sisterhood	Headlight	Moonwalk	Upright
Standout	Spacewalk	Turnaround	Whitewall	Skylark	Earring
Toothpick	Whitewash	Sometimes	Comeback	Daybed	

1. ANNUURORTD   T _ _ n _ _ _ u _ _

2. STHSEORIOD   S i _ _ _ _ _ _ o _

3. REDRAUNM   _ n _ _ _ _ _ m

4. SKALRYK   S _ _ l _ _ _

5. HWA LEITLW   _ _ i _ e _ _ _ _

6. LMWKOOAN   _ _ o _ w _ _ _

7. WBRENNO   N _ _ _ _ _ n

8. DUTTNAOS   _ _ a _ _ _ _ t

9. BAYDED   _ _ y _ _ d

10. IRENRGA   _ _ r _ _ _ g

11. KTTOIPH OC   _ _ o t _ p _ _ _ _

12. DOOW ODG   D _ _ _ _ o _ _

13. ITSEMESOM   _ _ _ e _ _ _ _ s

14. MCCBKAOE   _ _ m _ _ _ _ k

15. PCY UHKEN   _ _ y _ _ _ c _ _

16. TDAH LEGHI   _ e _ _ l _ _ h _ _

17. UDHREOABTN   E _ _ _ _ _ _ o _ n _

18. H IWHWSETA   _ _ i _ e w _ _ _ _

19. HSNOENIMO   _ _ _ _ _ h i _ _

20. EACLASWPK   _ _ _ _ _ w _ l _

21. SNNDUOW   S _ _ _ o _ _

22. SD WASNTEN   _ e _ _ _ _ a _ d _

23. RGIUTPH   _ p r _ _ _ _

Commonly Misspelled
Compound Words

Name: _____

Date: _____

Taxpayer	Carrack	Centercut	Upheld	Tailgate	Passkey
Dishwasher	Tableware	Throwaway	Anyplace	Playthings	Backslide
Foreman	Oneself	Uplink	Bluebell	Jetliner	Fishpond
Haircut	Handbook				

1. PTHNSIYGLA   P _ a _ _ _ _ n _ _

2. AKOHNOBD   _ _ _ _ _ o o _

3. SEDSAHRWHI   _ _ s _ _ _ _ h e _

4. UIKLPN   U _ _ _ n _

5. ACTHRIU   _ _ i _ _ u _

6. EAKLSCIDB   B _ _ _ _ _ i _ _

7. EEIJRNTL   _ e _ _ _ _ e _

8. ASSYKEP   _ a _ _ k _ _

9. TWLEBRAAE   _ _ _ _ _ w _ _ e

10. AYAPERXT   T _ _ p _ _ _ _

11. ITTALAGE   _ _ _ l _ _ t _

12. IPHODFSN   F _ _ _ _ _ _ d

13. LBUEBLLE   _ _ _ e _ _ l _

14. DHPLEU   U _ h _ _ _

15. RRCAKAC   C _ r _ _ _ _

16. PYCALEA N   _ _ _ p _ _ _ e _

17. OEENFSL   O _ _ _ e _ _

18. ENRMOAF   _ _ r _ m _ _

19. ARAT WHOYW   _ _ _ _ w a _ _ y _

20. ENTEURCCT   _ _ _ _ e r _ _ _

Commonly Misspelled Compound Words

Name: _____

Date: _____

Grandmother	Housetop	Waterspout	Newsprint	Afternoon	Moreover
Eyesight	Tableware	Shortbread	Grandson	Overshoes	Newsman
Comedown	Keyword	Weeknight	Goodbye	Noisemaker	Upset
Moonstruck	Tailspin				

1. CWMDEOON   _ _ _ _ _ _ w n

2. AENWSMN   _ e _ _ m _ _

3. ASGDR NNO   G _ _ _ d _ _ _ _

4. UEPST   _ _ _ _ t

5. OEMORE RV   M _ _ e _ _ _ _ _

6. DSOATBREHR   S _ _ _ _ b _ _ _ d

7. RDYEOW K   _ _ _ _ _ r d _

8. OEORSSHEV   _ _ _ r _ _ o _ _

9. AEONRFNTO   _ f _ _ _ _ _ o _

10. OERSTUPWAT   W _ _ e r _ _ _ _ _

11. RETPSWINN   _ _ w _ _ _ i _ _

12. EGETHIWNK   W _ e _ _ _ _ _ _

13. EEIYGHST   _ _ e _ _ _ _ t

14. ITNSPAIL   _ a _ _ _ p _ _

15. NIMRAEEOKS   _ _ _ _ _ m _ k _ r

16. CKNTOSORUM   _ o _ _ _ t _ _ _ k

17. HDTRONEGARM   _ r a _ d _ _ _ _ _ _

18. ABAETLERW   _ _ _ l _ _ _ _ e

19. GOYOBDE   _ _ _ d _ _ e

20. ETUHOSPO   _ o _ _ _ _ _ p

Commonly Misspelled Compound Words

Southwest	Background	Southeast	Horseplay	Tableware	Township
Pinstripe	Rainstorm	Highball	Fishhook	Bankbook	Weekend
Commonwealth	Bookcase	Wasteland	Takeout	Starfish	

1. B AKOOBNK   _ a _ _ _ o _ _ _

2. KGCDNBAOUR   B _ _ _ g _ _ u _ _

3. CABS OEOK   _ o _ _ _ a _ _ _

4. ESLANWTAD   _ a _ _ _ _ _ d

5. ASOSTTEHU   S _ _ t _ _ _ _ _

6. ITS RIENPP   _ _ n _ _ _ _ p e _

7. OSKHFOHI   _ _ s _ _ _ _ k

8. OAEUKTT   _ _ k e _ _ _

9. EKNEDEW   _ _ e k _ _ _

10. HNIT POWS   _ _ w n _ _ _ _ _

11. YEOSHARLP   H _ _ _ _ _ _ _ y

12. LHBHIAGL   _ _ g h _ _ _ _

13. EWU OTSHTS   _ o u _ _ _ e _ _ _

14. AIRSSTFH   _ _ a _ _ _ _ h

15. RNAMTORSI   _ _ _ _ _ t _ r _

16. REWAEABLT   _ _ b _ _ w _ _ _

17. OATMWOEMNLCH   _ o _ m _ _ _ _ _ _ t _

Commonly Misspelled Compound Words

Name: _____

Date: _____

Slumlord	Tablespoon	Newsbreak	Warmblooded	Uphill	Playboy
Forefinger	Timeshare	Tenfold	Baseball	Backlash	Earache
Snowball	Uppermost	Repairman	Bugspray	Watchmaker	Uproot
Wastebasket	Newsletter				

1. BAWMLROEODD   _ a _ _ _ l _ _ _ _ d

2. MEAARRI PN   _ e _ _ _ r _ _ _

3. DOEFTNL   _ _ _ _ o l _

4. LLMSDURO   _ l u _ _ _ _ _

5. PMETOPS UR   U p _ _ r _ _ _ _ _

6. ABKCSAHL   _ a _ _ _ a _ _

7. NWSOALBL   _ n _ _ _ a _ _

8. SATESTAEBWK   _ _ s _ _ b _ _ _ _ t

9. ASHIRTMEE   _ _ _ e _ h _ _ _

10. RSWE AENKB   _ e _ _ _ r _ _ k _

11. TNPLBOAESO   _ _ _ _ _ s p _ o _

12. HEACARE   _ a _ _ _ e

13. LIU PHL   _ _ _ _ l l _

14. CMKAWH RTAE   _ _ t c h _ _ _ _ _ _

15. GNEERRFFI O   _ o _ _ _ i _ g _ _ _

16. BALASLEB   B _ _ _ _ _ l _

17. OORTPU   _ p r _ _ _

18. TEEN LESTRW   _ _ w _ _ e _ _ e _ _

19. LOBPYAY   _ _ a y _ _ _

20. APSBYURG   B _ g _ _ _ _ _

Commonly Misspelled Compound Words

Name: _____

Date: _____

Alongside	Foothill	Elsewhere	Skintight	Upward	Fishbowl
Keypad	Stagehand	Deadend	Sunflower	Cabdriver	Newspaper
Telltale	Blackball	Earthworm	Pinhole	Snowbird	Skyscraper
Themselves	Foreleg	Waybill	Notebook	Crosscut	Horseman

1. UPWDAR   _ _ w a _ _

2. ADSTGEANH   _ _ _ g _ h _ _ _

3. PEYRSKSCRA   _ _ y _ c _ _ _ _ r

4. E PKYAD   _ e _ _ a _ _

5. VCBRDIAER   _ _ b _ _ _ v _ _

6. WLAYLIB   _ _ y _ i _ _

7. TSCUCROS   _ _ o _ _ _ u _

8. WFOLRNESU   _ _ _ _ l o _ _ _

9. HELWREESE   E _ _ _ _ _ _ r _

10. DWIBONSR   _ _ _ _ _ _ r d

11. ETSLVMSEEH   T _ _ m _ _ _ _ e _

12. LCABBALLK   _ _ _ _ _ _ a _ l

13. DDADENE   _ _ _ d _ n _

14. GHIISTKNT   _ _ _ _ t _ _ h _

15. NBOOEKOT   N _ t _ _ _ _ _

16. OTFILHLO   _ _ _ _ _ _ _ l l

17. OWHLISFB   _ i _ _ _ _ w _

18. S NOLADGEI   A l _ _ _ _ _ _ d _ _

19. SOHNREMA   _ _ _ s e _ _ _

20. FL RGOEE   _ o r _ _ _ _ _

21. A ELELTLT   T _ l _ _ _ _ _ _

22. OAWMRERTH   E _ _ _ _ _ _ r _

23. WESR NEPAP   _ e _ _ _ a _ e _ _

24. OINHPLE   _ _ n h _ _ _

Commonly Misspelled Compound Words

Name: _____

Date: _____

Fishtail	Northeast	Timetable	Fatherland	Forewarn	Drawbridge
Wastepaper	Upcoming	Forebear	Slowdown	Teamwork	Target
Newsworthy	Somebody	Turnaround	Teenager		

1. RHDNLFTAAE   F a _ h _ _ _ _ _ _

2. MTRAOWEK   _ _ _ m _ _ r _

3. TROTESA NH   N _ r _ _ e _ _ _ _

4. EGTTRA   T _ _ g _ _

5. TANDRNOURU   T _ _ _ _ _ o _ _ d

6. BEMTTEIAL   _ _ m _ _ _ b _ _

7. ILHFSATI   _ _ _ _ _ a _ _

8. EYSB DOOM   S _ _ _ _ _ y _

9. READGIBDRW   _ _ _ _ _ r _ d _ e

10. EEP SARATPW   _ a _ _ _ _ _ _ e _

11. NAERGT EE   _ _ _ _ _ _ e r _

12. NOUCGMIP   U _ _ o _ _ _ _

13. DLWOSOWN   S _ _ _ d _ _ _

14. ORAWFERN   _ _ _ e _ _ _ n

15. ERBFRAOE   F _ _ _ _ _ a _

16. SORWHNETWY   N e _ _ _ _ _ _ h _

Commonly Misspelled Compound Words

Name: _____

Date: _____

Butterball	Upstream	Cheesecake	Lifework	Airmen	Sandlot
Sharpshooter	Pinwheel	Crossbreed	Stonewall	Schoolbook	Underage
Upstanding	Waterfowl	Spacewalk	Lukewarm	Rainwater	

1. TEOLANLSW _ _ _ _ _ _ _ l l

2. EEA CHEKESC _ _ _ _ _ e _ a k _ _

3. RPOESOHASTRH _ _ a _ p _ _ _ _ t _ _

4. UBTETRLBAL _ _ t _ _ r _ _ l _

5. SCHOBKOLOO S _ _ _ _ _ o o _

6. MEAPRSUT _ p _ _ _ _ a _

7. ROREECBSSD _ _ o _ _ _ r _ _ d

8. RD ANUEGE _ _ _ e _ _ _ e _

9. AEUWKLMR L _ _ e _ _ _ _

10. ITRWEARNA _ a i _ _ _ _ _ _

11. ANEMRI _ _ _ m e _

12. TOSDALN S _ _ _ _ o _

13. PLAKCEASW _ p _ _ _ _ _ l _

14. KFELROIW _ _ _ _ w _ _ k

15. EATWRLFWO _ _ _ _ _ _ o _ l

16. TGDPISNUAN _ p s _ _ _ d _ _ _

17. HLPENEIW _ _ n _ h _ _ _

Commonly Misspelled Compound Words

Eyewitness	Cattail	Careworn	Turnoff	Warlike	Slapstick
Schoolwork	Sandlot	Textbook	Meanwhile	Shoelace	Turnbuckle
Foredoom	Undercover	Newsboy	Turntable		

1. PACKTSLIS   _ l _ _ _ _ _ _ k

2. TOADLNS   S a _ _ _ _ _

3. TFFRNUO   _ u r _ _ _ _

4. YOSNWEB   _ _ w _ _ _ y

5. HNMELIWEA   _ e _ _ _ _ _ l _

6. CAEEHOSL   _ _ o _ l _ _ _

7. YEWITSENES   E _ _ _ _ _ n _ _ s

8. N ECDVERURO   _ n _ _ _ c _ _ _ _

9. HCOOROS LKW   _ _ _ o o _ w _ _ _ _

10. RALUETBNT   _ u _ _ _ _ _ e

11. TATICAL   _ a _ _ _ i _

12. CRTBLEKUUN   _ u _ _ b u _ _ _ _

13. TOXTE KOB   _ _ x _ _ _ _ _

14. ARKWILE   _ a r _ _ _ _

15. CNWEORAR   _ _ _ e w _ _ _

16. MOORFDEO   _ _ _ _ _ o _ m

Commonly Misspelled Compound Words

Name: _____

Date: _____

Newscaster	Blowgun	Nursemaid	Rattlesnake	Forgive	Newsroom
Lifeblood	Watchword	Fishhook	Tenderfoot	Forehead	Granddaughter
Fishmonger	Waterfront	Forbid	Wheelchair		

1. FLLODIEO B   L _ f _ _ _ _ _

2. AECHLRIEHW   W _ e _ _ _ _ a _ _

3. KTNLEREATSA   _ _ _ _ _ _ n _ k e

4. RATRWOEFNT   _ _ t _ _ _ _ o _ t

5. NGLBWOU   _ l _ _ _ u _

6. OSHFOIHK   F i _ _ _ _ _ _

7. NGTGAEURDDHAR   _ _ a n d _ _ _ _ _ _ _

8. SRNW OMOE   N _ _ _ _ o _ _ _

9. HEOFGNISRM   _ i s _ _ _ _ _ e _

10. OEGFVIR   _ _ r _ i _ _

11. OBRIDF   _ _ _ b i _

12. ATCWHDWRO   _ _ _ c h _ _ _ _

13. FROHEDAE   _ _ _ _ h _ a _

14. EWCARTNSES   _ _ w _ _ _ _ t e _

15. UIDARNEMS   _ u r _ _ _ _ _

16. FTNRDEOOET   _ e _ d _ _ _ _ t

Commonly Misspelled
Compound Words

Name: _____

Date: _____

W	P	C	L	X	A	I	E	O	K	S	F	K	D	R	A	M	X	H	X
S	U	P	E	R	H	U	M	A	N	D	T	Y	O	E	R	V	X	A	T
C	W	S	U	P	R	I	S	I	N	G	E	R	W	A	C	F	W	N	G
Q	B	U	K	L	U	U	P	T	U	R	N	D	O	U	R	O	C	D	P
Y	U	P	C	X	P	K	E	Y	W	A	Y	U	E	N	B	W	I	M	B
H	T	E	A	S	P	U	R	J	S	C	T	S	Z	S	G	T	J	A	S
F	T	R	R	H	E	N	C	M	L	I	D	E	S	S	F	H	M	D	L
U	E	S	P	I	R	D	A	Z	I	M	T	O	L	K	O	T	O	E	B
C	R	E	E	P	C	E	R	J	F	J	R	E	G	L	H	J	P	L	T
O	S	N	T	B	L	R	S	Z	E	C	E	E	A	C	T	X	U	U	D
U	C	S	B	O	A	G	I	U	L	W	R	L	U	S	I	A	O	H	B
R	O	I	A	T	S	R	C	P	I	M	W	C	L	N	P	H	L	N	O
T	T	T	G	T	S	O	K	T	K	D	A	A	Z	Y	T	O	H	E	O
H	C	I	G	O	M	U	P	A	E	T	S	B	E	I	F	Y	O	V	K
O	H	V	E	M	A	N	H	K	F	D	H	D	W	P	B	I	M	N	M
U	A	E	R	O	N	D	T	E	N	F	B	R	I	Z	W	E	S	O	A
S	L	Y	L	R	A	I	L	W	A	Y	O	I	Y	D	O	D	L	H	R
E	S	U	P	E	R	F	I	N	E	Y	W	V	Z	I	Z	F	K	O	K
C	W	A	X	W	O	R	K	O	B	D	L	E	R	Q	W	N	E	N	W
N	U	F	O	R	E	G	O	N	E	I	O	R	C	A	N	N	O	T	I

Without	Upperclassman	Courthouse	Lifelike	Washbowl
Cabdriver	Butterscotch	Uprising	Teaspoon	Handmade
Railway	Jellyfish	Shipbottom	Stronghold	Upturn
Carpetbagger	Telltale	Below	Keyway	Underground
Waxwork	Crossbow	Uptake	Foregone	Superfine
Cannot	Superhuman	Supersensitive	Carsick	Bookmark

Commonly Misspelled
Compound Words

Name: _____

Date: _____

```
Q  V  W  F  O  R  E  S  H  A  D  O  W  T  T  J  S  W  B  C
U  N  D  E  R  B  E  L  L  Y  R  Y  L  I  H  F  T  P  L  R
B  A  L  L  R  O  O  M  T  E  E  L  P  M  O  Z  O  H  U  O
N  J  K  E  O  M  C  R  H  R  A  T  E  E  N  M  C  A  E  S
W  M  E  B  B  A  O  T  E  F  Z  A  X  K  E  B  K  W  G  S
A  P  C  T  N  P  A  R  R  M  S  P  F  E  Y  Z  R  R  R  W
O  C  Q  I  R  F  A  E  Y  O  P  R  K  E  B  M  O  L  A  A
W  Z  L  A  D  E  T  D  R  O  A  O  T  P  E  D  O  A  S  L
U  Y  C  N  B  A  O  C  I  N  C  O  W  E  E  V  M  U  S  K
R  K  A  E  W  B  U  C  C  L  E  M  I  R  Y  H  A  P  U  K
D  R  L  G  Y  Y  H  I  U  I  W  C  A  R  H  O  P  T  R  G
G  A  J  N  R  M  B  K  A  G  A  N  R  L  R  N  F  I  H  G
T  N  A  X  O  A  J  C  E  H  L  T  M  H  H  E  I  M  I  Y
V  S  G  U  C  R  N  E  O  T  K  Z  M  D  A  W  R  E  G  H
F  U  Z  N  B  H  U  D  A  M  L  S  V  R  N  S  E  Q  H  E
O  A  E  M  J  R  B  Z  C  R  E  B  A  W  D  P  H  D  L  R
S  P  E  A  R  M  I  N  T  H  D  B  C  T  O  R  O  O  A  S
T  E  N  D  E  R  F  O  O  T  I  R  A  L  U  I  U  A  N  E
W  S  C  H  O  O  L  B  O  Y  Y  L  U  C  T  N  S  S  D  L
H  U  N  U  T  C  R  A  C  K  E  R  D  M  K  T  E  S  B  F
```

Tenderfoot	Stockroom	Carport	Carhop	Nutcracker
Bluegrass	Crosswalk	Underbelly	Herself	Taproom
Spearmint	Highland	Foreshadow	Talebearer	Schoolboy
Eardrum	Newsprint	Anybody	Uptime	Firehouse
Grandchild	Timekeeper	Grandfather	Handout	Moonlight
Spacewalk	Ballroom	Honeybee	Waterfall	Comeback

Commonly Misspelled Compound Words

Name: _____

Date: _____

A	N	N	U	U	Z	T	G	R	A	N	D	U	N	C	L	E	T	F	Q
G	G	L	J	F	O	O	T	N	O	T	E	H	L	E	E	Z	U	F	M
Q	V	I	X	C	A	R	F	A	R	E	I	S	I	M	E	E	R	Q	X
I	M	C	G	U	R	A	I	N	B	O	W	L	I	N	T	X	N	L	L
R	B	W	H	I	T	E	F	I	S	H	E	T	D	I	S	N	B	I	E
J	S	F	O	R	E	M	O	S	T	E	R	R	B	Y	B	E	U	M	N
I	M	O	J	Z	L	L	N	I	H	I	A	K	A	F	C	W	C	E	H
S	T	E	M	R	M	S	D	W	A	O	C	W	S	Q	A	S	K	S	R
P	P	U	L	E	M	G	Y	Y	B	A	H	E	T	J	R	P	L	T	V
I	T	S	R	O	W	S	R	R	B	G	V	T	A	A	T	E	E	O	L
L	B	H	E	N	I	H	E	A	I	U	O	G	N	S	W	R	J	N	K
L	O	E	H	A	O	V	A	H	N	O	L	L	D	H	H	S	O	E	Z
W	U	E	D	D	O	F	R	T	R	D	Y	S	O	T	E	O	W	K	H
A	P	P	S	U	M	E	F	P	M	D	A	X	F	R	E	N	A	E	T
Y	S	S	H	P	P	O	A	Q	W	T	A	U	F	A	L	P	L	Y	Q
H	I	K	C	U	H	T	F	N	P	O	R	Y	N	Y	G	Y	K	V	M
A	D	I	S	L	H	A	N	D	C	U	F	F	B	T	K	P	W	R	P
G	E	N	T	M	Y	O	V	E	R	C	O	A	T	O	T	S	A	N	W
D	H	A	N	D	G	U	N	Q	W	G	G	W	J	O	O	H	Y	N	Y
K	W	D	M	H	T	K	V	U	P	M	A	R	K	E	T	K	S	B	Q

Overboard	Ashtray	Backbite	Turnoff	Spillway
Carfare	Daisywheel	Limestone	Handgun	Standoff
Granduncle	Grandaunt	Airtime	Handcuff	Upside
Whitefish	Daybook	Rainbow	Walkways	Turnbuckle
Newsperson	Foremost	Upmarket	Somewhat	Footnote
Overcoat	Sheepskin	Superhighways	Taproot	Cartwheel

Commonly Misspelled Compound Words

U	A	F	T	E	R	I	M	A	G	E	J	E	N	Y	U	L	M	J	M
H	W	G	R	A	I	N	C	H	E	C	K	C	X	S	F	P	Y	U	R
S	B	L	A	C	K	S	M	I	T	H	P	P	C	Y	V	Z	W	M	W
P	X	O	E	Q	H	E	A	D	A	C	H	E	J	M	U	R	Q	P	W
I	R	K	W	U	T	H	O	R	S	E	R	A	D	I	S	H	U	S	A
X	Y	S	D	L	T	H	E	V	I	W	A	Y	S	I	D	E	P	H	R
F	A	W	H	L	E	S	U	U	E	E	S	R	A	I	N	D	R	O	P
Z	W	F	H	A	N	G	U	N	A	R	N	H	T	Z	S	W	O	T	A
U	A	D	O	E	R	J	S	N	D	T	K	G	M	H	O	Y	A	B	T
W	T	R	A	O	E	E	K	U	R	E	I	X	M	T	Q	T	R	C	H
A	E	W	V	I	T	L	C	X	F	O	R	E	T	H	O	U	G	H	T
T	R	H	W	R	R	L	B	R	B	W	O	B	C	J	Y	R	A	M	E
E	C	E	P	L	X	Y	O	A	O	S	A	F	I	A	T	N	L	K	N
R	R	E	W	L	U	B	M	C	S	P	N	I	Y	R	Q	C	L	M	E
W	A	L	L	E	Y	E	D	A	K	E	P	R	N	D	D	O	O	P	S
O	F	H	F	A	H	A	D	W	I	E	A	E	W	Y	S	A	V	S	J
R	T	O	I	Q	F	N	T	B	J	D	R	B	R	S	T	T	E	D	R
K	Q	U	W	E	A	T	H	E	R	P	R	O	O	F	R	V	R	R	X
S	O	S	W	E	A	S	M	O	B	B	O	A	R	D	W	A	L	K	X
S	W	E	I	O	B	F	U	H	W	M	R	T	L	D	E	B	U	C	P

Wheelhouse	Walleyed	Wheelbase	Wayside	Raincheck
Thunderbird	Earthquake	Raindrop	Footlocker	Waterworks
Headache	Blacksmith	Allover	Jellybean	Dairymaid
Sharecropper	Takeover	Watercraft	Sunroof	Jumpshot
Fireboat	Bowlegs	Warpath	Horseradish	Forethought
Weatherproof	Afterimage	Turncoat	Boardwalk	Uproar

Commonly Misspelled Compound Words

Name: _____

Date: _____

P	W	U	T	A	R	G	E	T	W	R	A	H	K	W	L	E	O	W	D
H	A	R	N	E	W	F	O	U	N	D	B	W	V	E	R	G	N	G	Y
B	O	O	T	S	T	R	A	P	V	O	M	Y	E	A	E	A	P	E	M
Q	H	S	U	P	E	R	S	O	N	I	C	H	H	R	P	W	Y	A	G
D	H	E	B	O	O	K	W	O	R	M	W	S	E	E	Z	A	C	R	G
A	N	Y	R	D	G	R	W	A	E	R	E	P	C	M	D	T	L	S	L
Y	A	N	H	E	Z	W	G	Z	E	M	U	U	T	S	L	E	O	H	I
D	N	T	L	R	B	O	W	T	I	S	A	S	U	U	S	R	C	I	F
R	Y	F	M	P	F	Y	A	T	C	S	A	C	Y	U	D	M	K	F	E
E	M	O	A	D	H	W	O	S	R	C	R	H	L	P	P	E	W	T	T
A	O	R	L	R	L	H	Y	O	E	C	T	L	I	P	Q	L	I	Q	I
M	R	E	I	O	S	K	A	R	C	R	S	H	J	T	N	O	S	U	M
P	E	F	F	J	P	O	O	I	O	R	S	U	R	C	R	N	E	N	E
A	A	O	E	V	C	F	Y	W	R	D	W	O	U	P	S	T	A	R	T
N	R	O	S	A	K	B	E	B	N	L	P	R	G	G	P	F	V	S	Z
C	R	T	A	M	K	T	U	E	E	R	I	G	C	E	E	O	V	K	V
A	E	R	V	L	O	Q	I	J	I	A	F	F	O	N	E	T	I	M	E
K	E	P	E	N	D	R	P	A	B	J	N	L	T	T	J	X	S	E	T
E	T	F	R	T	F	T	D	S	R	M	C	B	O	L	D	F	A	C	E
N	K	V	J	U	S	U	N	L	I	T	S	H	A	D	Y	S	I	D	E

Hereby	Superego	Newfound	Soybean	Anymore
Supersonic	Gearshift	Shadyside	Target	Timeshare
Watermelon	Airlift	Forefoot	Bootstrap	Lifetime
Bookworm	Onetime	Airport	Pancake	Boldface
Friendship	Lifesaver	Saucepan	Sunlit	Waterwheel
Clockwise	Upstart	Noteworthy	Forecast	Daydream

Commonly Misspelled Compound Words

Name: _____

Date: _____

```
U  F  A  R  S  W  A  V  E  L  I  K  E  Y  U  K  R  N  Y  E
D  O  S  A  P  S  K  K  J  H  M  A  T  C  H  B  O  X  B  R
N  O  H  C  L  R  I  U  P  K  T  A  I  L  P  I  E  C  E  Z
T  T  O  Q  A  T  G  D  D  L  S  T  A  N  D  P  I  P  E  I
J  R  E  U  Y  A  M  S  E  P  A  C  E  M  A  K  E  R  Q  L
Y  E  M  E  H  B  S  F  K  K  E  A  R  D  R  O  P  N  X  Y
O  S  A  T  O  L  F  O  I  Y  I  Q  X  Q  K  O  D  U  A  G
U  T  K  B  U  E  C  I  M  S  L  C  Y  J  D  E  R  D  A  R
B  L  E  A  S  S  E  T  S  E  H  I  K  L  M  I  O  G  I  A
B  L  R  L  E  P  D  Y  B  H  H  B  G  I  Q  T  X  T  R  N
E  V  A  L  C  O  O  D  Q  L  H  O  O  H  T  A  R  A  C  D
D  S  M  C  U  O  S  I  B  V  A  O  W  W  T  W  C  K  R  N
C  N  C  C  K  N  X  A  T  D  M  C  O  B  L  I  M  E  A  I
L  A  E  U  Z  B  C  L  N  X  F  Z  K  K  N  P  T  O  F  E
O  K  P  K  A  I  O  A  P  E  T  X  G  O  I  N  A  F  T  C
T  E  X  F  X  U  H  A  U  Q  E  T  T  H  U  G  O  F  K  E
H  S  M  A  P  E  O  I  R  D  R  J  H  B  J  T  Y  W  L  S
E  K  T  Q  R  U  P  P  P  D  W  A  T  E  R  W  A  Y  E  W
S  I  W  O  H  E  A  D  D  R  E  S  S  J  E  T  P  O  R  T
A  N  F  P  X  F  O  O  T  B  A  L  L  K  F  N  Y  S  V  O
```

Somehow	Aircraft	Blackout	Today	Blackboard
Matchbox	Racquetball	Grandnieces	Tailpiece	Taxicab
Wavelike	Waterway	Footrest	Takeoff	Sidekick
Forehand	Jetport	Headdress	Standpipe	Playhouse
Skylight	Tablespoon	Snakeskin	Fishbowl	Shoemaker
Football	Fishhook	Bedclothes	Eardrop	Pacemaker

Commonly Misspelled Compound Words

Name: _____

Date: _____

```
O  J  F  D  L  R  N  E  W  S  D  E  A  L  E  R  W  F  D  O
L  I  M  E  L  I  G  H  T  F  I  R  E  B  R  E  A  K  C  F
R  T  F  O  R  B  E  A  R  E  R  S  T  E  A  M  S  H  I  P
H  C  I  S  O  U  N  D  P  R  O  O  F  B  A  T  Y  F  P  Z
O  O  U  N  G  E  D  T  A  B  L  E  C  L  O  T  H  T  F  Z
U  M  S  F  Z  T  A  X  J  J  I  H  O  U  S  E  B  O  A  T
S  M  K  O  O  V  A  S  U  N  B  A  T  H  E  N  E  P  U  S
E  O  A  D  R  R  Z  R  G  V  T  X  P  A  Y  R  V  Q  J  T
K  N  T  B  P  G  E  T  G  E  Y  U  C  G  O  J  D  B  I  A
E  P  E  J  M  T  D  S  R  E  C  R  N  T  V  L  N  A  K  N
E  L  B  M  M  I  Y  A  E  A  T  I  S  K  L  C  K  L  U  D
P  A  O  Y  C  L  W  G  E  E  K  K  S  A  B  O  A  L  P  B
E  C  A  E  C  T  O  T  K  A  O  G  Y  M  V  R  K  P  S  Y
R  E  R  G  F  D  Z  E  M  O  O  R  S  F  O  N  E  A  T  Z
N  F  D  O  R  W  M  S  B  D  R  J  E  N  Y  M  Y  R  R  O
K  Z  S  E  N  A  S  P  H  A  Y  W  E  G  S  E  H  K  O  V
B  K  D  K  C  A  J  C  C  A  N  Y  H  O  W  A  O  M  K  O
W  N  E  E  L  X  T  X  V  F  T  X  E  N  U  L  L  D  E  V
U  N  B  G  J  A  H  E  R  E  A  F  T  E  R  K  E  V  X  P
G  Z  B  E  W  M  H  O  N  E  Y  C  O  M  B  Q  L  T  T  W
```

Steamship	Commonplace	Upstroke	Keyhole	Watchdog
Teacup	Underdog	Became	Target	Sunbathe
Software	Firebreak	Houseboat	Housekeeper	Soundproof
Skateboard	Tablecloth	Standby	Honeycomb	Ballpark
Newsdealer	Bookstore	Limelight	Carryall	Foresee
Anyhow	Forbearer	Glassmaking	Hereafter	Cornmeal

Write a short definition in the box for each word

Upscale	Catwalk	Keyboard	Longhand
Woodshop	Forecastle	Coffeemaker	Undercurrent
Format	Wallpaper	Whitecap	Goodnight
Snowshovel	Turndown	Headline	Upstage
Teammate	Hamburger	Upthrust	Cheeseburger

Intake	Uppercase	Carload	Blacktop
Homemade	Tenfold	Brainchild	Eyelash
Underclothes	Wardroom	Newsbreak	Thunderbolt
Forefather	Backspin	Around	Dishcloth
Throwback	Someday	Washhouse	Waterline

Backspace	Crossover	Lifeguard	Widespread
Whatever	Washroom	Comedown	Sixfold
Aboveboard	Fishnet	Supergiant	Washcloth
Sweetheart	Turnabout	Eyecatching	Nowhere
Comeback	Sideshow	Softball	Upheaval

Turnbuckle	Another	Tenderfoot	Housework
Courtyard	Blueberry	Fireproof	Taillike
Caveman	Daisywheel	Showplace	Weatherman
Daybreak	Fireflies	Warfare	Blackberries
Basketball	Spokesperson	Grasshopper	Anyway

Teapot	Standpoint	Therefore	Tagalong
Underachieve	Upkeep	Sunday	However
Backstroke	Washout	Daylight	Upon
Scarecrow	Nevermore	Dishwater	Showoff
Forklift	Teaspoon	Carefree	Riverbanks

Raincoat	Doorstop	Driveway	Butterfingers
Longhouse	Lifeline	Waistline	Thunderstorm
Sailboat	Bellbottom	Horsehair	Fruitcup
Horsefly	Washtub	Update	Upwind
Grandparent	Underdevelop	Taskmaster	Backbone

Hammerhead	Someone	Eyeballs	Together
Bedrock	Watershed	Underfoot	Playback
Keystone	Because	Mainline	Tailgate
Tapeworm	Backhand	Washrag	Supercargo
Waterpower	Cardboard	Blacklist	Hookup

Eyelid	Daytime	Sundial	Wheelbarrow
Grassland	Snowbird	Afterlife	Salesclerk
Inside	Newsreel	Moonscape	Lifelong
Takeout	Honeysuckle	Mothball	Candlestick
Blackmail	Underestimate	Steamboat	Grandnephew

Brainwash	Uptight	Butternut	Something
Uptown	Airfield	Bedroom	Carpool
Rubberband	Dishpan	Storerooms	Dairymaid
Superstructure	Superhero	Sunfish	Egghead
Wastewater	Keynote	Superpower	Eggshell

Wipeout	Firecracker	Deadline	Supercool
Cabdriver	Weekday	Waterscape	Weathercock
Highchair	Forever	Stepson	Meantime
Household	Afterglow	Lifeboat	Tabletop
Wavelength	Ironwork	Bluebird	Mainland

Spelling Test

Your Answers
1
2
3
4
5
6
7
8
9
10
11
12
13
14
15
16
17
18
19
20

Correct Spelling If Incorrect
1
2
3
4
5
6
7
8
9
10
11
12
13
14
15
16
17
18
19
20

Spelling Test

Your Answers

1 _____
2 _____
3 _____
4 _____
5 _____
6 _____
7 _____
8 _____
9 _____
10 _____
11 _____
12 _____
13 _____
14 _____
15 _____
16 _____
17 _____
18 _____
19 _____
20 _____

Correct Spelling If Incorrect

1 _____
2 _____
3 _____
4 _____
5 _____
6 _____
7 _____
8 _____
9 _____
10 _____
11 _____
12 _____
13 _____
14 _____
15 _____
16 _____
17 _____
18 _____
19 _____
20 _____

Spelling Test

Your Answers

1
2
3
4
5
6
7
8
9
10
11
12
13
14
15
16
17
18
19
20

Correct Spelling If Incorrect

1
2
3
4
5
6
7
8
9
10
11
12
13
14
15
16
17
18
19
20

Spelling Test

Your Answers

1 _____
2 _____
3 _____
4 _____
5 _____
6 _____
7 _____
8 _____
9 _____
10 _____
11 _____
12 _____
13 _____
14 _____
15 _____
16 _____
17 _____
18 _____
19 _____
20

Correct Spelling If Incorrect

1 _____
2 _____
3 _____
4 _____
5 _____
6 _____
7 _____
8 _____
9 _____
10 _____
11 _____
12 _____
13 _____
14 _____
15 _____
16 _____
17 _____
18 _____
19 _____
20

Spelling Test

Your Answers	Correct Spelling If Incorrect
1	1
2	2
3	3
4	4
5	5
6	6
7	7
8	8
9	9
10	10
11	11
12	12
13	13
14	14
15	15
16	16
17	17
18	18
19	19
20	20

Spelling Test

	Your Answers
1	
2	
3	
4	
5	
6	
7	
8	
9	
10	
11	
12	
13	
14	
15	
16	
17	
18	
19	
20	

	Correct Spelling If Incorrect
1	
2	
3	
4	
5	
6	
7	
8	
9	
10	
11	
12	
13	
14	
15	
16	
17	
18	
19	
20	

Spelling Test

Your Answers

1
2
3
4
5
6
7
8
9
10
11
12
13
14
15
16
17
18
19
20

Correct Spelling If Incorrect

1
2
3
4
5
6
7
8
9
10
11
12
13
14
15
16
17
18
19
20

Spelling Test

	Your Answers
1	_____
2	_____
3	_____
4	_____
5	_____
6	_____
7	_____
8	_____
9	_____
10	_____
11	_____
12	_____
13	_____
14	_____
15	_____
16	_____
17	_____
18	_____
19	_____
20	

	Correct Spelling If Incorrect
1	_____
2	_____
3	_____
4	_____
5	_____
6	_____
7	_____
8	_____
9	_____
10	_____
11	_____
12	_____
13	_____
14	_____
15	_____
16	_____
17	_____
18	_____
19	_____
20	

Spelling Test

Your Answers

1
2
3
4
5
6
7
8
9
10
11
12
13
14
15
16
17
18
19
20

Correct Spelling If Incorrect

1
2
3
4
5
6
7
8
9
10
11
12
13
14
15
16
17
18
19
20

Spelling Test

Your Answers	Correct Spelling If Incorrect
1	1
2	2
3	3
4	4
5	5
6	6
7	7
8	8
9	9
10	10
11	11
12	12
13	13
14	14
15	15
16	16
17	17
18	18
19	19
20	20

Spelling Test

Your Answers	Correct Spelling If Incorrect
1	1
2	2
3	3
4	4
5	5
6	6
7	7
8	8
9	9
10	10
11	11
12	12
13	13
14	14
15	15
16	16
17	17
18	18
19	19
20	20

Spelling Test

Your Answers

1 _____
2 _____
3 _____
4 _____
5 _____
6 _____
7 _____
8 _____
9 _____
10 _____
11 _____
12 _____
13 _____
14 _____
15 _____
16 _____
17 _____
18 _____
19 _____
20

Correct Spelling If Incorrect

1 _____
2 _____
3 _____
4 _____
5 _____
6 _____
7 _____
8 _____
9 _____
10 _____
11 _____
12 _____
13 _____
14 _____
15 _____
16 _____
17 _____
18 _____
19 _____
20

Spelling Test

Your Answers

1

2

3

4

5

6

7

8

9

10

11

12

13

14

15

16

17

18

19

20

Correct Spelling If Incorrect

1

2

3

4

5

6

7

8

9

10

11

12

13

14

15

16

17

18

19

20

Spelling Test

Your Answers	Correct Spelling If Incorrect
1	1
2	2
3	3
4	4
5	5
6	6
7	7
8	8
9	9
10	10
11	11
12	12
13	13
14	14
15	15
16	16
17	17
18	18
19	19
20	20

Spelling Test

Your Answers	Correct Spelling If Incorrect
1	1
2	2
3	3
4	4
5	5
6	6
7	7
8	8
9	9
10	10
11	11
12	12
13	13
14	14
15	15
16	16
17	17
18	18
19	19
20	20

Class: _____

Day	Week:					Week:					Week:					Week:				
	M	T	W	Th	F	M	T	W	Th	F	M	T	W	Th	F	M	T	W	Th	F
Date																				
Assignments																				
1																				
2																				
3																				
4																				
5																				
6																				
7																				
8																				
9																				
10																				
11																				
12																				
13																				
14																				
15																				
16																				
17																				
18																				
19																				
20																				
21																				
22																				
23																				
24																				
25																				
26																				
27																				
28																				
29																				
30																				
31																				
32																				

Week	Monday	Tuesday	Wednesday	Thursday	Friday
1					
2					
3					
4					
5					
6					
7					
8					
9					
10					
11					
12					
13					
14					
15					
16					
17					
18					

Notes _____

Made in the USA
San Bernardino, CA
24 July 2020